The World of the White-tailed Deer

A LIVING WORLD BOOK
Editor: John K. Terres

The World
of the White-tailed Deer

TEXT AND PHOTOGRAPHS BY

LEONARD LEE RUE, III

J. B. Lippincott Company

Philadelphia and New York

To My Beth

Contents

Author's Introduction

THIS BOOK is the culmination of years of observation of the white-tailed deer in the field. I have read about them and photographed them at every opportunity. Today, almost everyone has the chance to study deer at first hand, since they can be found practically everywhere in the United States. This is a recent development, however. I am fortunate to have lived most of my life in an area that has a tremendous deer population. Deer are my closest neighbors and about tenfold more numerous than their human counterparts. Fascinated by all things in nature for as long as I can remember, the study of deer has been a never-ending quest of mine.

Many of the things I have written about in this book are the observations of men who have studied the deer and recorded their findings before me. No one man's life is long enough, nor his powers of observation strong enough to have seen all these things for himself. I can only hope that in some small measure the many personal things I have seen and here recorded will be helpful to others.

I would like personally to acknowledge and to thank all of the many people who have helped me through the years in my work with deer, but to do so would make an almost unending list. I believe that it is almost impossible to come in contact with a person without learning something from him.

I want to extend my thanks to virtually every game commission in the United States for sending me all the data and information that they had available. In particular, Will Johns of Pennsylvania, and C. W.

The World of the White-tailed Deer

Severinghaus, Jack Tanck and Eugene McCaffrey of New York have helped immeasurably.

Two personal friends who have made possible much of what I have done are Fred Space and Joseph Taylor. I can only hope that they know how much I appreciate what they have done for me.

It has been a great pleasure and an extensive education to work with John K. Terres, my editor, a friend of many years' standing. Together, we have tried to make the reading of this book both educational and enjoyable.

And though my wife, Beth, knows how much I appreciate her translating my scribbling into a typed manuscript, I also want the world to know it.

LEONARD RUE, III

Columbia, New Jersey
April, 1962

The Deer Itself

WHAT IS a deer? A deer is many things to many people. To the farmer it is a nuisance, to the forester it is a plague, and to the motorist a hazard.

The deer is classified scientifically in the phylum Chordata because it has a backbone; in the class Mammalia, because it is warm-blooded, has a four-chambered heart, a covering of hair on its body, gives birth to its young alive, and has mammary glands with which to nurse its young. The deer is in the order Artiodactyla, meaning even toes, because it has four toes on each foot, and the entire deer family is known as Cervidae. The particular deer that we are going to talk about in this book is known as *Odocoileus virginianus*.

The deer is the number-one big game animal in the United States and a challenge to hunters everywhere. Its value, both aesthetic and monetary, to individuals, communities, and states is so great as to be almost beyond computation. Millions of people thrill to the sight of deer and it is for them as well as anyone else interested in deer in any manner that this book has been written.

It has been well established that a deer will spend most of its life in an area composed of about one square mile. The deer's intimate knowledge of every topographical feature in its home range is the key to its ability to survive during the periods of danger encountered in the hunting season. It is also almost impossible to drive a deer out of its home range and, if evicted, it will return at the very first opportunity.

I know of one buck, live-trapped by New Jersey's wildlife men, that

The World of the White-tailed Deer

was removed from the Celanese Company's land at Belvidere and released at Mt. Lake, a distance of about six miles. The buck returned home, clearing the eight-foot fence to get back in, and was retrapped within a week. He was then released at Dunnfield Creek, a distance of eleven miles, and again he returned home. His third release was made in the southern portion of the state, a distance of about one hundred miles, and this time he never returned.

Because deer love apples, these are the most common bait used in the live traps. Some deer overcome their fear of the traps and can be caught almost daily in the same trap in their effort to get their favorite food. The record for being retrapped in one spot probably belongs to a deer in Michigan that, during the winter of 1936, was caught fifty times in a three-month period.

White-tailed deer are not migratory in the true sense of the word. Caribou, elk, or even mule deer, on the other hand, may travel great distances. The white-tail does make occasional shifts of its home range to a more sheltered area in winter to "yard," if forced to do so by the elements. However, this seldom means a move of more than a few miles. The greatest distance traveled by the white-tail in migration, recorded by George Shiras, involved a distance of about seventy-five miles. These deer retreated from the western end of Michigan's Upper Peninsula each winter because of lack of food and moved down into Wisconsin. In order that their fawns could be born on the summer range, the does would be in the vanguard of the returning deer each spring. The bucks followed along later at a much more leisurely pace. This is the established pattern for almost all migratory animals.

By 1870 the deer's migration pattern had altered, mainly because much of the virgin timber had been cut off and the area soon grew sufficient deer browse to support the herds in the wintertime.

That deer resist the impulse to migrate is demonstrated by the fact that large numbers have starved to death rather than leave a yarding spot to move even a few miles to an area where there may be abundant food.

A doe browsing on dogwood shoots.

The World of the White-tailed Deer

Many states have conducted extensive trapping programs in which the deer were tagged or belled and then released or transported elsewhere in an effort to establish home ranges and migratory patterns. The conclusions reached were that the weather, much more than either food or water, determines why a deer moves and how far it will travel to seek the shelter it needs.

One of the first lessons to be learned about going into the woods either to study deer or to hunt them is that almost everything is in the deer's favor. It all boils down to the simple fact that deer have constantly to use their senses for survival and we do not. Consequently, they usually see, hear or smell us and are gone before we are even aware that they have been in the area.

Deer are color blind, seeing the world in monochromatic tones and shadings of gray. Because of this the bright red or yellow of a hunter's jacket does not lessen his chances of success. Deer do not appear to see an object that does not move or, if they do, are not concerned about it. However, the slightest movement will be seen immediately, causing the

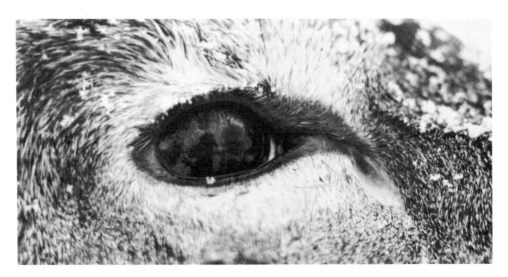

The preorbital gland in front of the deer's eye acts as a tear duct.

4

deer to focus its eyes upon the object that has moved. The deer will then "freeze" and intently study whatever has attracted its attention. Even the blinking of a human eyelid can be enough to send the alerted deer streaking off to safety.

The deer's ancient ancestors had five toes on each foot. Although we think of a deer's hoof as its foot, we must remember that it is in reality its toenails. It is thought that five toes hampered the speed of prehistoric deer. They could not run easily to escape their enemies. Through evolution, the first toe, corresponding to our thumb, disappeared completely. The second and fifth toes, corresponding respectively to our index and little fingers, shrank in size and moved to the rear where today they remain as dewclaws. The third and fourth toenails slowly enlarged and formed the hoofs, as shown below.

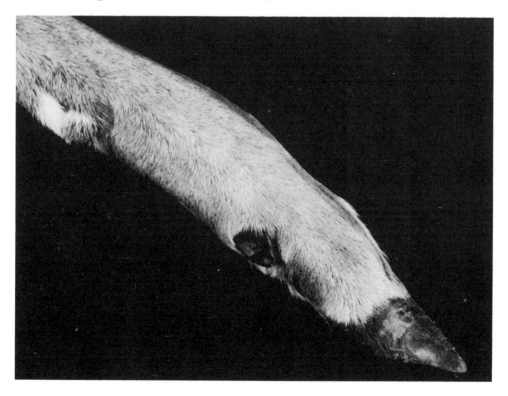

The World of the White-tailed Deer

These hoofs give the deer a very good grip on hard ground, the type of terrain they most frequent, and to a lesser extent, on rock surfaces. In most deer, the center portion of each hoof has retracted so it is not exposed. However, I examined not long ago a foot from a buck just killed by a hunter in which the center portion was fully extended as is the mountain goat's hoof. This softer padding would have given a very good grip on even a steep rock face.

Deer have great difficulty walking or running on ice and if chased to a frozen lake or river by dogs, wolves, coyotes, or human hunters, they are practically doomed. If the deer slips and falls down, it is almost impossible for it to arise. Deer rescued after falling on ice often die because of exhaustion brought on by their efforts to get up.

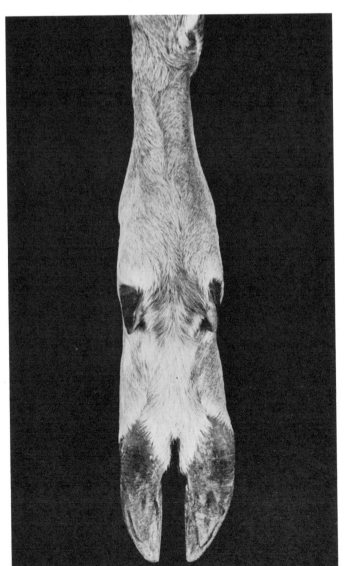

A deer's hoof from the underside, showing hard outer edges and softer inside area.

The Deer Itself

The sharp hoofs of deer are also used by them as weapons in fighting, or for protection. While a deer may kick with its hind feet, it is much more likely to rear up and strike out with its forefeet. A blow from the forefoot could easily crush the skull of a dog or coyote. Striking its adversary a glancing blow, the deer's hoof may tear and cut the flesh of its foe.

Although most deer seem to fear snakes, there are many recorded instances of does attacking and killing poisonous snakes, to protect their fawns. The doe usually approaches the coiled reptile carefully, then leaps into the air and comes down repeatedly on the snake with all four feet held together. The sharp hoofs effectively cut the snake to ribbons and offer it a very small chance of being able to bite the doe.*

Many hunters have been seriously injured by approaching a deer that they thought was dead only to be struck by flailing hoofs as the deer regained consciousness.

There is much argument and conjecture as to whether you can tell the sex of a deer by its hoofprints. Many hunters claim that they can, although I have never seen satisfactory proof of their ability. It is claimed that a buck's hoofs will be broader, heavier, and more rounded at the tips than those of a doe because a mature buck will be larger than a mature doe. The opposite seems to be true, however, in my home state of New Jersey, where it is estimated that few bucks ever get to be over two and one-half years old, most of them being killed before maturity. Since does in New Jersey are protected, they may reach the ages of ten and twelve years. A doe of this age is going to have a broader, more rounded tip of the hoof than will a buck of perhaps one and one-half years of age. In many cases the doe will also outweigh the young buck, and her hoofprints will sink a little deeper in the soft earth. The dewclaws of both sexes show only when the ground is exceptionally soft and the hoofs sink deeply, so that these marks are also ruled out as a means of telling the difference between the sexes. The dewclaws of deer,

---

* Woodsmen and charcoal-burners of the southern New Jersey pine barrens have told me that they have watched deer (both bucks and does) kill rattlesnakes in this way.—ED.

7

incidentally, were highly prized by the American Indians and were used by them both for ornamental wear, such as in necklaces, and in the making of dance rattles.

The only reliable trail mark I know of is found after a slight snowstorm of one inch or less. Here the buck's hoof tracks will be accompanied by a drag mark while the daintier doe will pick her feet clear and leave just the hoof mark itself. This holds true for moose tracks also. In both species, the buck's drag marks become more pronounced in the rutting, or mating, season.

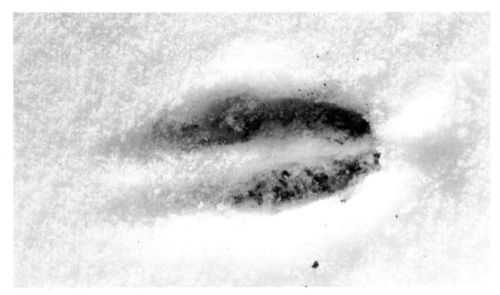

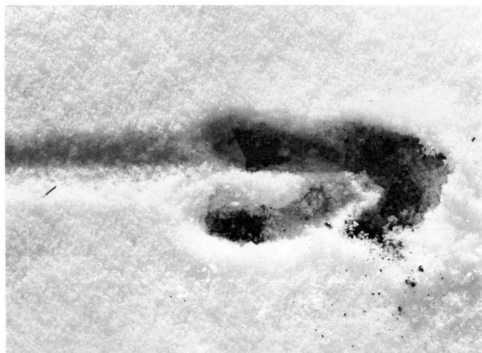

In this light snowfall, drag marks are clearly visible, indicating that a buck and two does have walked together here.

The World of the White-tailed Deer

A buck does not grow antlers during his first year. He has small knobs where his future antlers will grow. These knobs at times are so small that they can hardly be felt and are best located by the two swirls of hair growing on the spot where the antlers will develop. At other times they may be raised up as much as three-fourths of an inch. In this condition the buck is known as a "button buck."

In the buck's second year, when he is sixteen to eighteen months old, he will probably develop spikes. These are usually straight, smooth, unbranched antlers that may measure one inch long or may be eight to nine inches long, although the average length is four to five inches. I have seen a buck with long, smooth, curving spikes fourteen inches long, but this is exceptional. Of course a buck in this stage is known as a "spike buck." A buck feeding under ideal food conditions will skip the "spike" stage and go on to develop much larger antlers.

A button buck, below, with antler tips just visible above the swirls of hair. At right, a spike buck.

The Deer Itself

A buck in his third year, or at thirty months of age, will usually have antlers that will branch. Then he is known as a "rack buck," and now develops a striking difference between the antlers of the white-tailed buck and that of the mule deer buck.

A white-tailed deer has branches, tines, or points developing from two main antlers, one on either side of the head. These main antlers are called beams. There is much controversy over what constitutes a tine or a point. In some sections of the country a point or tine was any piece of protruding antler large enough to support the strap on a pair of binoculars. This was a very poor system, as some malformed racks had so many points that they resembled a cactus. As many as seventy-six points have been found on some freak antlers. These antlers usually result from an internal or external injury to the deer. The practice today is to consider a point as any protruding piece of antler at least one inch in length.

At left, a four-point, crotch, or "Y" buck; the rack buck below has antlers with more than four individual points.

The World of the White-tailed Deer

Whereas the white-tailed buck develops single points from the main beam, the mule deer develops Y's from the main beam. Because of this it is a very simple matter to tell the species apart.

When the white-tail's antlers first branch he is known as a "four-point," "Y," "prong," or "crotch" buck. From this stage on the buck is known by the number of points or tines that he develops. Eight points is the average number on a good head, although an eight-point buck may have very small antlers while a six-point buck may have very large antlers. This, again, is a result of the relative nutritional value of each deer's food. Some of the record bucks have as many as thirty-seven good legitimate points.

Many people try to tell the age of a buck by his antlers. This cannot be done. Even scientific measuring of the diameter of the base of the antler has not proved very accurate. Antler development is not an indication of age but of nutrition and the amount of food consumed. A buck getting lots of nutritious food can develop from a button buck in his first year into a rack buck of many points in his second year. This has been proved repeatedly by various states on game farms where the animals kept in captivity were fed different kinds of foods. An old buck, past his prime, may revert to four points, spikes, or even become what is known as a "muley," bearing no antlers at all. This condition is brought about by hormone deficiency, because of increasing old age.

The most accurate method of discovering a deer's age is by the examination of its lower teeth. This has been perfected by C. W. Severinghaus and Jack Tanck of New York State's Wildlife Laboratory at Delmar. Improving upon studies by previous workers and making more complete collections of the lower jawbones of deer, these men have followed the lead of a new method, which is probably an outgrowth of the observations used since the earliest times by horse traders the world over.

It surprises people unfamiliar with the dentition of a deer to find that, like cattle and other ruminants, they do not have any front teeth

12

This rack buck's antlers have eight points, or tines.

on the upper jawbone. Instead, they have what could best be called a tough resilient "pad." Because of this absence of upper teeth it is easy for the trained observer to differentiate between the rough chewed twigs nipped off by deer and the "knife-cut" twigs removed by rabbits, for example.

A deer with a fully developed set of teeth has a total of thirty-two. In the upper jaw, it has six premolars and six molars; in the lower jaw, six incisors, two canines, six premolars, and six molars. The canine teeth of deer resemble incisors to such a degree that they are usually classed together with them.

The fawn is born with eight incisors or front milk teeth. Sometime after the first week, four premolars develop with another pair shoving through after four or five weeks of age. The first molar usually erupts through the gum at about three months, the second molar at about six months, and the third molar completes the set at about nine months.

At seventeen months the three-cusped cap of the third premolar is pushed out and replaced by a two-cusped tooth. Recently, a friend of mine returned with a six-point buck he had killed in Maine. He told me that the guide had claimed the buck was six and one-half years old. Upon examination of the deer and using the Severinghaus charts I was able to prove that the buck was seventeen months old instead of six and one-half years. The third premolar was just losing the immature three-cusped top. From this age on, the average person must use charts or have known specimens at hand for comparison in order to age deer because after the age of seventeen months tooth wear is the only reliable guide.

Other factors affect tooth wear at this point. A deer living in a sandy section of the country will pick up more abrasive material while feeding and its teeth will wear far more quickly than will those of deer in other areas. Then, too, many of the specimens of jawbones used for comparisons are from pen-raised, or captive deer which did not feed upon normal browse but on softer commercial feeds and therefore did

At right, lower jawbones showing the development and wear on teeth of deer aged, from bottom, 1½, 2½, 3½, 4½, 6½, 7½, 9½, and 11½ years.

Below, jawbones from deer aged, from bottom, 6 months, 9 months, and 1 year, showing additional molars taking their place as the deer advances in age.

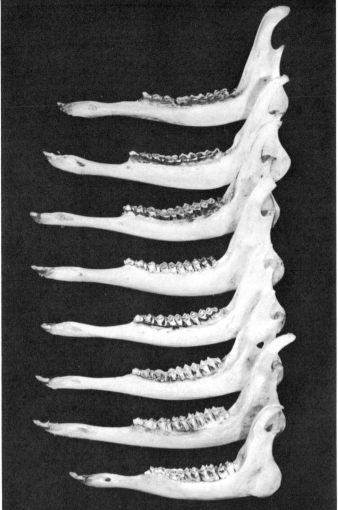

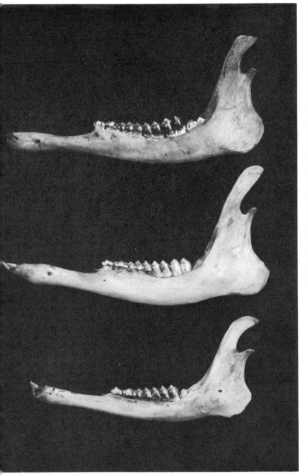

Photograph at right shows typical wear on teeth of 2½-year-old deer (below) and extreme age, at 11½ years.

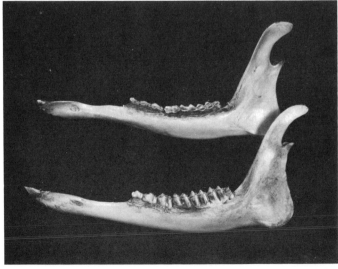

not have normal tooth wear. A third factor is that of ample food and nutrients. Healthier deer have the better teeth.

Each one of the four sections in a deer's stomach has a different shape, capacity, and lining. The rumen, or main storage stomach, will hold eight to ten quarts of food. The lining consists of small spaghetti-like papillae varying from three-eighths to one-half inch in length. There are about 1600 of these papillae to the square inch.

The second part of the stomach is known as the reticulum. This section looks like a honeycomb and can hold material about the size of a softball. Real digestion starts to take place in the omasum or the third stomach. This chamber has about forty-eight flaps of various sizes, four inches long and one and one-eighth inches high, which act as strainers. The last portion of the stomach is called the abomasum and is very smooth and slippery.

An adult deer has about sixty-five feet of intestines. It takes from twenty-four to thirty-six hours for food to pass completely through them.

Deer also share with other ruminants the odd habit of swallowing indigestible material. In some of the stomachs I have examined, of deer killed or starved, I have found numerous small stones, a .22-caliber bullet case, and even a piece of melted glass.

Deer, like many of the other plant feeders, do not have a gallbladder on their liver; it is not needed. Acorns probably contain more fats than any other food deer consume, yet they apparently have no trouble digesting and assimilating them without the aid of the gall secretions.

From personal observation of hundreds of deer, I have found that they masticate each piece of their cud with an average of forty chews. The largest number of chews I ever witnessed was fifty-two, the smallest twenty-three. The average forty chews take about forty-five seconds. This masticated cud is then reswallowed and a new one regurgitated. It requires from six to eight seconds for the one cud to go down and the next cud to replace it in the mouth. This passage of the cud is easily visible even at quite a distance. Each cud is about the size of a lemon in

bulk. On many occasions, I have held my hand on the throats of tame deer and felt the passage of the cud. The number of cuds that a deer masticates during one period depends entirely upon the length of time that the deer is undisturbed. Because of the frequency with which a deer moves about, it is unlikely that the paunch is ever entirely emptied of cuds.

The averages cited above are based on deer feeding upon natural browse. Deer feeding upon softer foods, such as farm crops or commercial feed, may have less chewing to do to prepare their food for absorption.

According to my research, the heaviest white-tailed deer on record was a buck that weighed an estimated 425 pounds live weight. It was shot by Albert Tippett near Trout Lake, Michigan, in 1919 and had a dressed weight of 354 pounds. In the forty-odd years since there has not been another deer to equal this record.

Of the various species of white-tailed deer those of the northern forests are generally the largest while those of the South and Southwest are smaller, with the Key deer of Florida being the smallest. Bucks are larger than does at birth, and remain so throughout their lives.

The average adult buck weighs from 175 to 200 pounds; an adult doe weighs from 30 to 40 pounds less. Many bucks weigh over 200 pounds, although one weighing more than 300 pounds is rare. It must be remembered that deer are not fully mature until three and one-half or four and one-half years of age and, as I have pointed out, the average life expectancy of a buck is far less in heavily hunted areas.

The size of a deer is often baffling to a novice. In the woods a live deer seems to be a large animal. From measurements I have taken I find that about thirty-four inches shoulder-height is average for does, and the bucks are three to four inches higher; a buck measuring forty-one inches at the shoulder has been recorded. Deer vary in over-all length from sixty to seventy-five inches according to the species, with the northern white-tail in the seventy to seventy-five inch class.

Spring

IT IS spring. Almost everywhere over the wide range of the white-tailed deer in North America—from Canada to Mexico and from the Atlantic Ocean to the Rocky Mountains—it is the birthing time of young deer. It is the period of warmth and new life—of green, newly-leaved forests and the richness of nesting birds and the hum of insect life; the fragrance of wildflowers, mingled with that of sweet grasses. It is the time when the does are heavy with the weight of their unborn fawns.

At the time of giving birth, does, still accompanied by their fawns of the previous year, attempt to lose them or drive them away. The yearlings are baffled by the belligerent attitude of the mother who had so carefully guarded and guided them through their infancy. At last, after repeated rebukes, not knowing why it must be so, they leave the doe, and she is free to seek the solitude she needs.

The birth of the fawn may be in some spot carefully chosen by the pregnant doe or, as it seems more often, wherever she is when her time arrives. Fawns are born in thickets, open grassy fields, woodlands, swamps, and other places with little indication of forethought by the doe.

As the moment of birth arrives, a sense of urgency dominates the doe, and she becomes very restless. With heaving flanks and opened mouth, she lies down, then arises only to lie down again. Her body strains and her movements aid in her labor. In a normal birth, the forefeet of the fawn appear first, followed quickly by its head. The fawn, during birth, is in a position suggesting someone about to dive into the

19

water. The entire birth may require only ten minutes, or it may consume an hour.

A doe giving birth for the first time will probably have only one fawn. From that time on, until extreme old age, twins will be most common—if food and living conditions are favorable. Triplets are fairly common, quadruplets are known, and there are at least two records of quintuplets.

There is usually a lapse of between ten minutes and an hour between the births of twins. The second birth is invariably easier.

Immediately after their birth, the doe gives her fawns a thorough washing by licking them with her rough tongue. She seems aglow with pride and as anxious as a human mother to be certain that her baby is perfect, as she goes over each fawn inch by inch. The young are by this time attempting to stand. The washing by the mother deer is usually so vigorous that it knocks the unsteady little fawns off their wobbly feet.

As soon as it is possible for the fawn to walk a few steps, the doe will lead it away from its place of birth. The doe wishes to leave the area before a predator is attracted to the spot where the fawns were born. In their early attempts at walking, the fawns' legs seem much too long. Although they can stand in less than ten minutes, it takes about an hour before they gain some semblance of control, and can walk.

In the beginning, while nursing, the fawns have difficulty in reaching the doe's udder, and usually do so while the doe is lying down. The difficulty is due to their unsteadiness on their feet and not to the shortness of their legs. Whenever one of the twins nurses, it usually becomes a signal for the other one to do likewise. The doe's udder has four nipples, therefore she could nurse quadruplets simultaneously. The fawns punch and pull at the doe with great force in their eagerness to feed. They are capable of drinking eight ounces of milk in less than a minute, but it is not likely that the doe can supply that much because of the frequency with which the young deer feed.

Still wet, this newborn fawn tries out his long, wobbly legs.

21

The newborn fawn finds it easier to nurse while the doe is lying down.

A good mother, the doe licks and washes her fawns as they nurse.

As the youngsters nurse, they quiver all over with excitement and wag their short tails vigorously. Small amounts of milk mix with their saliva and this becomes whipped into a foam that makes the fawns appear to be frothing at the mouth. The doe usually licks the fawns with her tongue while they nurse.

A fawn, except for the nursing period, is inactive for the first three or four days of its life. Its spotted coat is a wonderful camouflage and allows the fawn to blend into almost any background. The fawn knows instinctively that it must remain motionless when danger is near. At such times, while lying down, it usually puts its head upon the ground and flattens its ears against its neck, thus reducing its total visible body bulk. Tests made in the field have indicated that the fawn is further protected at this time for a period of three or four days by being odorless. Dogs have been known to walk downwind of a newborn fawn and to be unable to detect its presence. Other predators would have similar difficulty in detecting the fawn by smell.

At this time the doe stays away from the fawn as much as possible to prevent her own body scent from giving away the fawn's location. She returns to nurse her young eight to ten times in a twenty-four-hour period. After the fawn has nursed, the doe makes it lie down. She may do this by voice or, if the fawn persists in following her, she may force it to lie down by pushing upon the youngster with her head or one of her forefeet. I once watched a doe force her young one down in this way.

Once, a few years ago, I was taking a series of photographs of a nesting red-eyed vireo and was working from a bird blind. The blind was made of canvas and burlap on a framework of wood. I had discovered the vireo's nest when it contained only one egg, the first of four to be laid. I immediately moved my blind into the area and each day for a week I moved it a little closer to the nest until at last I had it in the proper position. I was operating my camera by a remote-control air bulb. As I wanted a complete set of photos of the nestlings, I took pictures from the blind early every morning for thirteen days. Secure in the blind, I could observe all that went on outside by looking through the mesh of the burlap yet no creature could look in and see me.

I had entered the blind before daybreak and was unaware of the single fawn which lay in front of the blind about seventy-five feet away. Suddenly a doe stepped into sight. I was hidden in my blind, and watched her excitedly. What was she doing there? After cautiously testing the air with her nose, she walked over to the fawn which I now saw for the first time as it bounded up to greet her. After briefly touching noses, the fawn started to nurse and when it had finished, the doe started

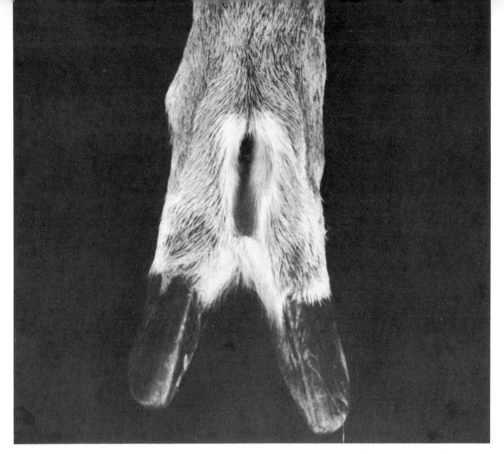

The interdigital gland in the deer's hoof secretes a substance which leaves a scent, by which the doe can track her fawn if it wanders off.

to leave. The fawn followed. Again and again the doe turned and swept the fawn back by pushing against it with her head. The fawn persisted until at last the doe raised her forefoot, placed it on the fawn's back, and pressed it to the ground. At this, the fawn lay still, and the doe passed out of my sight.

When people discover a small fawn lying out in the fields or woodlands, they are likely to come to the conclusion that it is an orphan or one that the mother has lost. Little do they realize that the doe is probably watching them from some nearby thicket. The doe seldom goes out of earshot of the fawn's blatting call. As the fawn grows older, it may occasionally wander off, but the doe can easily locate it by means of a telltale track of scent left by glands located between the hoofs on the fawn's feet, which discharge a waxy secretion.

Although it is better for a person finding a fawn not to handle it at all, the doe will not abandon her baby because some thoughtless human has touched it. Deer are not panicked by the scent of man because nowadays they live in or near populated areas where the scent of man, although it may mean danger, is commonplace to them.

All too often, the person who takes a fawn home with him is not capable of giving it the proper care, and no matter how good that care may be, it does not begin to measure up to the care that the mother could provide. When the deer grows up, especially if it is a buck, it can be dangerous, particularly in the rutting, or mating, season. In addition, the game laws of almost every state prohibit the removal of young deer from their natural haunts.

After a period of about three to four days, the fawn's hoofs, which were soft and well blunted during the period the doe carried her young, begin to dry and harden, and the undersurfaces to retract.

The doe may not allow the fawn to follow her while she is feeding until it is about three weeks old. By this time, the fawn has good control of its legs and can outrun the average man. The fawns grow rapidly on the rich milk provided by the mother. Deer milk is very similar to that of the reindeer, which has about three times as much protein and butterfat as does our finest Grade A cow's milk.

The added drain of nursing her fawns in May, after nourishing them in the unborn state through the previous winter months when food was scarce, reduces the doe to an emaciated condition. To add to her unkempt appearance, her long winter hair is sloughing off in big patches. To aid in this shedding, the deer will often pull this old hair out by the mouthful.

The month of May affects not only the doe but the buck. This is the period when his antlers start their yearly growth. The increasing amount of daylight hours of spring has a tremendous impact upon the world of nature. This is known as photoperiodism, and it causes birds to seek their ancestral nesting ground in the north, animals to shed their hair (and many to change colors), and is responsible for many of the other seasonal phenomena of wildlife.

The increased daylight is picked up by the eyes of the adult buck deer and transmitted to the pituitary gland at the base of the skull. The pituitary gland then stimulates the release of testosterone. That this hormone is the main factor in controlling antler growth has been proved. An overabundance of the same hormone in a doe will cause her to grow antlers too. Almost every state that allows the hunting of deer has reported these antlered oddities, and it has been estimated that they occur about once to every 18,000 normal bucks.

The pedicel, the base from which the antler starts to grow, has been covered with a layer of skin since the previous antlers were shed earlier. As the testosterone acts upon the deer's body, this skin starts to swell, due to calcium deposits forming the antler. The velvet, as this network of veins is called, is nothing more than a kind of modified skin.

The new antlers are among the fastest-growing forms of animal tissue known.

The World of the White-tailed Deer

It nourishes the antler from the outside, instead of from the center as in the growth of true horns such as cattle have. The antlers at this time are pliable and easily damaged. The buck seems to realize this and takes great care not to strike them against trees or other hard objects. The antlers bleed readily because all the veins are on the surface. They are hot to the touch and covered with short bristly hair.

If the young buck gets the proper nourishment, his antlers develop rapidly.

"You are what you eat" is an old saying pointing up the need for a balanced, nutritious diet. This also holds true for a buck's antlers. Any buck that gets a diet of nourishing browse of twigs and bark containing the needed amounts of calcium and phosphorus will grow an impressive set of antlers. A young buck requires about twice the amount of protein and nutrients that an adult, three-year-old buck needs. An adult buck grows the largest antlers. The young buck's requirements are for body growth, and then antler development, whereas the adult buck, having reached maturity, no longer has the drain of body growth.

A buck in velvet feeding upon staghorn sumac, so called because its stalks and branches are velvety like young antlers.

With the coming of summer, the warm weather brings a season of plenty. New plant growth and sprouts of all kinds abound now. The deer eagerly feed upon the budding maple, sassafras, oak and willow trees, blackberry, blueberry, sumac bushes, and sweetfern. Deer, which never have a large individual range, now travel less than ever.

Those deer living adjacent to farm lands, as the bulk of our deer do, are quick to supplement their woody plant browse and are frequently seen now feeding in the fields. Extensive damage is done by them when the deer concentrate on a particular crop. Farm crops such as celery, cabbage, and lettuce are especially vulnerable. Corn, clover, buckwheat, alfalfa, and other regular farm crops they also eat in large quantities.

Each year, I plant about forty acres of various food plants especially for wildlife. The soybeans never even get started. The deer swarm to the fields as soon as the first bean growth appears, and every sprout is nipped off. Any growth the bean makes through the day is eaten the following night. After about ten days, the beans are beaten in the unequal struggle. Commercial raising of soybeans in my area is an impossibility. Even corn can only be raised in fields completely enclosed by deer-proof fences.

Now that the hunting season is past, the deer feed more in the daytime, especially the early morning and evening hours. They seldom leave the fields before eight in the morning and are back again to feed at five in the afternoon of the same day. Before the coming of the white man, deer fed almost entirely during daylight. The continuous pressure of man and his activities has forced them to become more active at night.

Corn eaten by deer. Note the track.

The World of the White-tailed Deer

Today, periods of deer activity can be read as an accurate short-range weather forecast. When deer come out of hiding and start to feed earlier in the day than usual, it foretells a dark and probably stormy night. On a moonlit night, the deer will start to feed later but will remain more or less active all night and retire to their thickets with the dawn.

A deer requires about ten to twelve pounds of food each day, which it can gather in one to two hours. As we have seen, a deer is a ruminant; that is, having four stomachs, it eats first and chews later. This is of tremendous protective importance. It allows an animal that is preyed upon, such as a deer, to expose itself away from its protective cover for the shortest possible time. In the early days of our country when there were many native predators—the cougar, the lynx, and the wolf—the deer would slip out from cover, eat quickly and then retire again into hiding. Today, after filling its first stomach, or rumen, the deer, instead of going back to the cover of swamps or woodlands, often lies down right out in the fields.

A doe lying out in the field, peacefully chewing her cud.

Summer

LATE SUMMER is a time of quiet for the white-tailed deer. The sun beats down and heat rises from the parched earth. The grasses are drying and brown and the leaves of trees and shrubs hang listless in the shimmering heat. It is a time of ease and reduced activity among many animals, and some, like the chipmunk and other ground squirrels, escape the prolonged heat and dryness of August by withdrawing into their burrows in the cool earth. There they lie in a somnolent state, called aestivation, or "summer sleep," and they may remain in their burrows for days at a time. Songbirds now feed early in the morning before the hot sun has started its daily march across the glaring skies. Many birds are molting, and remain hidden in the woods and brushy hillsides. These are the so-called dog days of August. All wild things adjust to the heat as best they can.

Now the fawns of the white-tailed deer lie beside their mothers in the shade on hillsides where stray breezes may be set in motion. With their mouths open and tongues exposed, they pant rapidly. This expulsion of air causes their bodies to rock in constant motion. Not able to perspire as humans do, the deer keep cool by pumping body heat through their blood and into the lungs, where it is drawn off by their rapid breathing. Their coats of hair are thin and coolly efficient. The doe has completely shed her winter coat and for the past several months she has worn a sleek red summer coat of which the hair is short, thin, and straight. Its main disadvantage to the doe is that it offers her little in the way of protection against the myriad hordes of biting insects that are

36

the constant companions of all animals that live in the woodlands at this season. Blood-sucking flies, mosquitoes, and midges are the principal attackers and they swarm to the bodies of living animals that furnish them with a meal of blood. These are parasites because they live at the expense of another animal, deriving their food, and sometimes protection, from their host. Usually parasites are harmful to the animal they live upon, either in causing it great annoyance or, occasionally, even in causing its death.

It is at this season that the female nose botfly starts a new cycle of life for her future progeny by crawling up the nostrils of deer and laying her eggs on the deer's nasal membranes. When the tiny botfly larvae hatch, they move deeper into the nasal passageways, where they grow to about one inch long. The following spring, the larvae crawl back down the nostrils and fall to the ground where they develop into an adult botfly in about two months. The cycle is started again when the adult botfly lays its eggs in the nostrils of another host deer. Although these parasites do not seem to do the deer actual body harm, they must cause them considerable torment.

About four o'clock in the afternoon, the deer bestir themselves from their siesta, and wander down to whatever bodies of water are in their area. Small ponds are particularly favored by them but they also frequent lakes and rivers. The deer drink deeply of the water and then commence to feed on plants that grow in the pond waters—water lilies and others. The adult deer often wade out up to their bellies to feed but the fawns seem to lack this confidence and prefer to feed and frolic in the shallows. When the deer eat water lilies and pondweeds, they also ingest tiny aquatic snails which are clinging to these plants. The snails are hosts to larvae of the liver flukes, another parasite of deer. When these larvae reach the deer's stomach, they crawl to the liver, which they enter and there grow to maturity. The adult flukes then lay eggs which are passed out of the deer's body and hatch in water. These microscopic larvae then seek out the necessary water snails and their life cycle as a

The World of the White-tailed Deer

parasite has begun.

Deer like water. Many times I have watched them feed for hours in a small pond located a few miles from my home. They apparently need water to get relief from biting insects, as do moose. Water is also a haven of safety from predators because here the longer-legged deer have the advantage, if they choose to stand off an enemy, by wading into deep water and then striking at their pursuers with their forefeet. Or the deer may simply swim to safety by going to an island, or crossing a river. There are several islands near my home that does will swim to in the spring in order to have their fawns in the seclusion and safety that the islands offer.

A doe (opposite), up to her knees in water, feeding on horsetails, rushes, and sedge.

The World of the White-tailed Deer

The deer-hunting seasons in Pennsylvania and New Jersey are separated by about two weeks, with Pennsylvania's first. Herds of deer numbering up to seventeen or eighteen are often seen jumping into the Delaware River from the Pennsylvania side; they swim across to the safety of New Jersey, only to swim back two weeks later when the New Jersey season opens, and the Pennsylvania side is quiet.

Deer have been clocked at speeds of up to thirteen miles per hour in the water and have traveled distances of up to five miles. However the white-tailed deer is not a strong swimmer, and if molested while in the water, it will become panicky and soon drown. Deer also have a tendency to bog down easily in mucky spots because of the slenderness of their hoofs and legs.

Below, and on the next three pages, a sequence taken at high speed, showing how a deer rises, when it can do so leisurely: first to its foreknees, then to its feet, then stretching comfortably to get the kinks out.

Summer

I believe that part of the appeal of the white-tailed deer is its seeming embodiment of all that is graceful, whether in motion or standing still. Everyone who frequents the haunts of deer is familiar with the graceful explosion of their flight. A deer surprised from its bed seems determined to take a long journey in as short a time as possible. This impression is heightened by the deer's speed of about thirty to thirty-five miles an hour over terrain on which we, as humans, find it difficult merely to walk. However, this headlong flight is of short duration. As soon as a hill, swamp, or suitable clump of trees has been placed between it and whatever created the disturbance, the deer stops. The white-tail is a skulker and prefers to accomplish its objective by stealth rather than speed. Deer can maintain speeds of thirty to thirty-five miles an hour for short distances, but an average of twenty to twenty-five miles an hour can be sustained much longer.

When a deer lies down, it first goes down on the knees of its forelegs. Then it lowers its hindquarters to the ground, and rolls to one side so that its body is completely touching the ground. When arising, it reverses this procedure; lifts itself to its foreknees, raises its hindquarters, then stands up from its knees, using one leg at a time to raise its fore-

quarters. This of course describes a leisurely arising. When startled, the deer bounces up so fast that all four legs are used simultaneously.

A deer running at full speed bounds with body-arching ground-covering leaps. The forefeet touch the ground first and then the powerful hindquarters come down with the back feet landing ahead of the spot where the front feet touched. By the time the hind feet have touched the ground, the body has already bunched itself and is uncoiling like a released spring. Some of these leaps will cover from twenty-eight to thirty feet. I don't know how high a deer could jump if forced to, but I have seen one clear an eight-foot-high fence from a standing position.

I have also seen deer jump through fences that they could easily have jumped over. Some of the fences had barbed-wire strands a foot apart yet the deer slipped between the strands and seldom touched them.

At one time the deer became so numerous in the fenced-in area surrounding the Hercules Powder Company at Belvidere, New Jersey,

A deer bounding through the woods at full speed.

A deer can clear obstructions more than eight feet high with ease.

that it was decided to hold a "deer drive" to force them out of the en-closed area. Accordingly, a large section of the fence was removed and about 150 of the local people turned out as drivers. A well-known fact was soon brought to light. You may stir deer up and get them moving, but you can't drive them. They go where they want to. One of the first deer to be seen jumped directly over the head of one of the drivers and another panicked and ran right over another driver, knocking him down, breaking his glasses, and cutting him up considerably. I was next in line to the unfortunate driver and am convinced that the deer never

44

even saw him in its headlong dash for safety.

At last, a large portion of the herd was moving toward the area where the fence had been removed. I saw numerous deer jump the eight-foot fence from both running and standing positions. Many of the deer ran smack into the fence because of the pressure of the drivers. The next day several of the deer were seen leaping the fence to get back home.

Deer also gallop: one forefoot comes down after the other forefoot has landed and is about to be lifted to take the next stride. In trotting,

A white-tail fawn leaping over a rail fence, showing how the feet and legs are placed as the body hurtles forward.

45

A deer trotting.

deer lift opposite feet fore and aft while supporting the body with the other two. When moving to and from their feeding grounds, deer either trot or walk, saving their speed for emergencies.

Another gait is known as single-footing. This is used only by a deer made either suspicious or nervous by something it cannot quite comprehend. At such times, with every nerve and fiber alert, the deer is the very essence of beauty. Lifting one of its forefeet parallel to the ground as if to stamp it, the deer will start to trot. Instead of bringing the foot

46

down to make the step, it holds it in the air while the other forefoot makes two steps. Then the raised foot is lowered and the other one held up for two steps. This gait is made awkward only by my poor description of the beauty of the actual movement.

Perhaps one of the main bonds of interest between man and the other mammals is that most of them enjoy playing too. Deer, particularly the fawns, show their zest for life by gamboling about in much the same manner as lambs do. They run, jump, butt at each other, chase objects such as butterflies and grasshoppers, and have a thoroughly good time doing it. Even the yearlings and occasionally the older deer have sham battles in which they rise up and lightly strike at each other with their forefeet. The deer have their own version of leapfrog and often jump over each other. All such play is a conditioning for actual life and serves an essential and useful purpose.

The sense of smell plays a very important role in a deer's world. I have often stalked them only to be betrayed by a shift in the wind which carried my scent to them. I believe that, on level ground, a distance of perhaps one-third of a mile would be the maximum range that scent can be carried, and detected by deer. Distances longer than that would allow too many variables to destroy the scent, for example rising thermals of air, cross-drafts, and other odors which might be picked up along the way. Deer are very much aware of the importance of the wind direction and take advantage of it at every opportunity. If at all possible, they prefer to feed facing into the wind. Thus, while concentrating on food, they have a much better chance of detecting an enemy by scent. It is because of the practice of heading into the wind that deer do not feed in one spot until all the available food is consumed. By taking a bite here and a mouthful there and walking always into the wind, the deer are constantly putting more distance between themselves and any predator that might also be taking advantage of the wind and stalking

47

them from the rear, or downwind, side.

In the daytime, the deer like to be up on the ridges of the hills and mountains. This allows them more relief from the flies in summer, but it is also a habit practiced most of the year. By being near the top of the hill there is very little chance that a predator can come over the top without the deer hearing the danger. As the smallest amount of sunlight will start heat thermals of air rising, the scent of anything below the deer will be wafted up to their sensitive nostrils to be classified. At night the deer feed in the lowlands where another well-known law of physics aids them. As air cools, it settles, bringing to the deer in the valley the scent of any living animal on the hillsides above them.

Frequently the deer, particularly a wise, mature buck, will head into the prevailing wind before walking in a circle preparatory to lying down for the day. By circling back toward his trail, the buck can lie down and watch his backtrack. In this way he can see if anything is following him, and still be secure, in that the wind blowing from behind him will warn of any unseen enemy in that direction.

Besides good eyesight and an acute sense of smell, deer also have an extremely keen sense of hearing. The large ears of a deer are as sensitive as a radar antenna and are constantly twisting, turning, scanning, and screening the air for any possible sound of danger. No sound seems too slight to escape them, and I am sure that hearing is one of the deer's most highly developed senses. I have discovered that deer hear best in the higher registers of sound. It is much easier to get the attention of a distant deer by squeaking with your mouth than it is by snapping your fingers if the volume of both sounds are the same.

Deer not only listen to the natural sounds of the woodland but also to the sounds made by the other woodland inhabitants. The alarm-cawing of crows, the chattering, scolding voice of the red squirrel, and the piercing call of the blue jay are all recognized as danger signals that accurately pinpoint the presence of something strange, and the possibility of its being danger. The deer heed all these warnings.

The ears of the deer are continually in motion, picking up signs of danger. The cawing of crows can send a deer bounding for cover.

The World of the White-tailed Deer

In hunting deer, drives are sometimes put on in which one group of hunters walks through the woods in a line in an attempt to push the deer ahead of them so that the standing hunters can get a shot. Most of the time, the drivers make all the noise possible by shooting, yelling, and even beating on pots and pans. The noise thus created often works for the deer instead of against them, as it allows them to pinpoint the exact position of each of the drivers. Knowing where each man is located gives the deer a chance to hide or else slip through the line where no driver is present.

Deer are at a distinct disadvantage on drizzly days when all the leaves in the forest are damp and soundless, allowing the hunter to get close to the deer before they can discover him. A windstorm also works against the deer, making them very nervous and alert because of the constant crashing of dead limbs falling to the ground; the whipping of branches and brush, coupled with the swirls and eddies of the wind, effectively rob them of the advantages of both smell and hearing. At such times, deer seek out the thickest cover possible in heavily forested ravines or swamp thickets.

Perhaps our greatest lack of knowledge concerning wildlife is in animal communication. The voice of a young fawn has been compared to the bleating of a lamb. As the fawn grows older, its voice sounds more calf-like but lacks the volume and depth of sound. One winter day, I rescued a young buck deer weakened by starvation that bawled as I approached him and kept right on as I carried him out of the woods. I was raised on a farm and am familiar with the sounds of domestic animals, and I can only say that the deer sounded exactly like a calf.

I have heard both bucks and does blatting with a rather toneless sound much like that an old ram sheep would make. The artificial calls sold to hunters today, as aids to hunting, are designed to imitate this sound. They are effective too, as I have called deer with a homemade caller. The does call more often than the bucks, which for the most part

50

remain silent.

A sound uttered by deer more frequently than by other animals is a snort of apprehension when startled. The snort, or "blow," may be likened to a greatly magnified sneeze, and is produced by a large amount of air being expelled through the deer's nostrils with great force. This snort may serve a dual purpose. Mucus is blown from the deer's nose by the pressure, which possibly opens up the nostrils so that the deer can more readily test the air by smelling, and the sound may startle the deer's opponent into moving thus giving away its location.

I well recall one of the first times I heard a deer snort. I was about fourteen years old and had been out that evening. Walking home along the back country lane without a light, I was not thinking about deer. Suddenly, out of the darkness, came a loud, explosive snort that set my heart pounding. Somebody was out there in the darkness and I wondered who it was. I was walking along a cutback lane that was below the surface of the surrounding fields, which were about at my eye level. Even though there was no moon, objects in the field were silhouetted against the low skyline. Off in the distance, to my great relief, I saw a buck and a doe stop running to look back in my direction. As the breeze was blowing toward me, the deer had no idea what I was when I had startled them. Back they came, step by cautious step, until at last they caught my scent, when they bounded away again, snorting at every jump. Although the deer may have been satisfied to have identified me, they could have no idea how glad I was to have been able to identify them.

Deer also communicate by stamping their feet much as rabbits do. While the rabbit thumps with his hind feet, a nervous deer stamps with its forefeet. Although this sound can be heard, it can probably be felt for a much greater distance through the vibrations of the earth. The deer will lift its forefoot very slowly and gracefully, pause a second, and then stamp downward with great force. It will do this repeatedly when disturbed.

A deer stamps its forefoot not only out of nervousness but as a means of warning other animals of the approach of danger.

The World of the White-tailed Deer

Although the pronghorn antelope of the western United States is usually referred to as the "heliographer," it is not alone in the ability to flash signals by flaring the white hair on its rump. The white-tailed deer also does this much more than most of our mammalogists realize.

Everyone is in agreement that the name "white-tailed" is most appropriate for this deer. As they bound off through the woods, they usually hold their tails aloft and display the white underside as proudly as a banner. With the white hairs erected and the tail bouncing loosely from side to side, it makes a very conspicuous splash of white. This show is not for our benefit, no matter how much we enjoy it. The flashing tail is the beacon that guides the doe's fawns as they run after her in the dimly lighted forest. Bucks generally do not raise their tails as they run.

One of the first actions taken by a deer that has just discovered

something suspicious is to flash its tail, or flare out the white hair on its rump. As deer are particularly observant of the slightest movement, this flashing will alert the entire herd in a moment, even though no sound has been made by the alarmed deer.

The hair on a deer's rump is about three inches long. When the brown hair overlaps the white hair and the tail is clamped down, very little white can be seen. By flaring out the rump hair so that the white is dominant, the deer can enlarge the white area as much as twelve additional inches. By moving the muscles controlling the hair, the white area can be flared at will and, if facing the sun, will cause flashes that can be seen as far as a mile.

Sometimes the use of its tail signals are to the deer's disadvantage. In stalking a feeding deer with a camera, I always watch the tail. Before a deer raises its head to look around, it always twitches its tail. When this happens, I stand absolutely still. Not seeing any motion, the deer resumes feeding, which gives me a chance to move closer. The whole secret of when to move and when to stand still can be read in the movements of the deer's tail.

Curiosity is a sign of intelligence even though it often gets animals into trouble. However, curiosity may be useful to a deer in its world.

Deer are intently interested in anything that they do not understand. Many times I have surprised deer that would not run away until they had circled and caught my scent. They just wanted to know what they were running away from.

A deer approaching an unknown object is a study in contrasts, as the photographs on the following two pages show. Torn between fear and curiosity, one part of the deer's being urges it to run away, while another urges the deer onward. With carefully placed steps, to assure a good foothold if speed is needed, the deer advances, neck outstretched and head lowered, with ears pointing forward. Its body may tremble under the pressure of nervousness and taut muscles. At last, the deer finds that everything is all right and accepts the object or else it discovers

55

The World of the White-tailed Deer

that something is wrong and no time is to be lost in making good its escape.

One of the main reasons for the present expansion of the range of the white-tailed deer, is its adaptability, fostered by its curiosity, which stimulates deer to eat new foods and to live under new conditions.

With the exception of those killed in the hunting season, more deer are probably killed by automobiles than in any other way. States with large deer populations, such as Michigan, have a yearly highway kill of over 6,000 while even small states such as New Jersey have over 2,000 deer killed this way each year.

Even these numbers, as high as they are, are conservative because they are based on deer actually reported and picked up by state game officers. Many, many deer struck by automobiles are not found because the deer is able to get off the highway and into the brush before it dies. Then, too, many deer hit by cars aren't reported.

A deer crossing the highway—just in time.

Summer

New Jersey loses a larger percentage of its deer to highway accidents than Michigan because of New Jersey's more extensive network of roads, the heavier traffic on these highways, and the diversity of crops that lure deer across the roads. The deer herds in rural New Jersey are tremendous attractions to the people in adjacent towns and cities, and many people drive into the country to watch the deer feed.

Deer browse along the roadside in spring because plant life turns green there first and in the greatest profusion due to the reflection and retention of heat by the paved roads. A doe killed at this time means the destruction of three deer as her unborn fawns die with her.

Although accidents probably cause the death of a relatively insignificant number of deer, they have all kinds of misfortunes, just as humans do. While reaching high for food, their necks and forelegs sometimes get caught tightly in crotches of trees, where they die a tortured death of pain and starvation. They run into woven wire fences and become entangled in the meshes; break through the ice of lakes, ponds, and rivers, and drown; are trapped on ice floes and swept away from land; get impaled on the branches of trees while running; fall over cliffs and are dashed to death on the rocks below; fall into wells and silo pits; get mired in muck or quicksand around the edges of swamps, rivers, and marshes; are struck by lightning; poisoned by herbicides—all this as well as being struck and killed by trains and automobiles.

In addition deer are susceptible to both internal and external parasites—deer lungworm, the cattle lungworm, stomach worms, tapeworm, footworm, lice, mites, and ticks. Wounds or injuries become infected, abscesses develop, and some deer have skin tumors.

Some deer are born blind and, of course, usually do not live long. Of eight congenitally blind fawns discovered in Wisconsin, six had opaque corneas in both eyes. Another fawn was born without any eyeballs, another had no irises in its eyes; another no lenses; another, tumors on the cornea.

In the summer, deer feed in the fields and may cross and recross highways to get to them. A doe killed shortly after the birth of her fawns means that the fawns also die because it is exceedingly rare that another doe will adopt and nurse the orphans. As the fawns grow older and follow their mother to feed, they are more susceptible to being hit on highways as they lack the co-ordination and knowledge of an adult deer in getting out of an automobile's way.

Deer at night are both attracted and blinded by car lights and, after jumping into the road, may stand immovable before the onrushing car. It is usually a safe bet that if a deer crosses the road ahead of your car then you had better slow down as there will probably be two more deer following her, if not more. A doe is almost always followed by her new fawns or the yearlings. If a family group is split like this, one group is going to cross or recross the road in order to stay with the other. If you are aware of this, it can save the lives of a lot of deer and prevent repair bills for your car.

A deer weighing 125 pounds hit by a car traveling at 50 miles an hour can cause the car great damage. A friend of mine had the main framework of his car so badly bent that it was practically ruined and had to be towed away. Another deer jumped from a high bank onto the hood of a car owned by a friend and crashed through the windshield. In the ensuing crackup, the car front was demolished and the driver hospitalized.

In August, the fawns, although still nursing, are varying their diet by eating plants. They usually nibble experimentally at plantains and orchard grass when about one week old and continue to eat larger amounts as they get older. This lessens the strain on the doe considerably. At birth, a female fawn weighs about five pounds, and a male seven pounds. On its rich milk diet, a fawn gains rapidly until by August it weighs about thirty pounds. Although it is usually weaned by September, I have seen fawns that had lost the spotted coat of the young deer try to nurse in November. Most fawns wean themselves, but those that

Although this fawn is large enough to live on plant food, the doe still allows it to nurse.

do not are hastened along by the doe. When one tries to nurse she will refuse to stand still, and if the fawn attempts to nurse from the rear by sticking its head between the doe's hind legs, the doe walks off. If the fawn nurses from the side, the doe will either turn her body in the opposite direction, or will walk away. Sometimes she may even lift her near leg right over the fawn's head, which effectively pushes the young one away when the leg is brought down. Occasionally a doe will "baby" her fawn, allowing it to nurse for a much longer period than is usual. As

The World of the White-tailed Deer

there seems to be no other explanation for this, human parents will perhaps feel better in knowing that they are not alone in indulging their children.

By the end of August a buck's antlers are fully grown. If they have not been damaged or injured, the two sides will probably be symmetrical. But injury to the buck's body while the antlers have been developing may also cause malformation, as shown in the photograph. If, for example, a buck is injured on its left side, the left antler will be misformed. Whether the body injury causes actual nerve damage affecting the left antler, or whether it is the buck's turning his head to lick the injury, thus putting pressure on the tender antler, that causes the malformation is not known.

Summer

As the growth of the new antler is completed, a cluster of cells forms at the base and grows outward, effectively shutting off the blood supply. Without blood, the velvet that covered the tender new antler soon dries, and commences to peel off. This apparently causes the buck to experience the same itching that we have when our sunburned skin starts to peel. We find it almost impossible not to scratch to relieve the itch, and the deer does the same thing. A buck frequently bends his head back and scratches his antlers with his hind foot.

The velvet on the buck's antlers (above) was shed in a single night. Right, the same buck several days later, a few scraps of velvet still hanging from his polished antlers.

The World of the White-tailed Deer

By the middle of September, the bucks have started to rub their antlers against small saplings and bushes and to scrape off the velvet-like covering. Mature bucks in good condition will frequently peel their antlers clean in a single night, while others may take a week or more, giving them the appearance of being festooned with Spanish moss. I have seen young spike bucks take as long as three weeks before they could actually free their antlers of this sheath of dead skin.

The velvet has begun to peel off this buck's antlers, showing one dry, bare tine.

Autumn

THE HUNTER'S moon hangs low in the sky, a thin silver crescent shedding soft light on the silvery earth below. Crisp, golden, exhilarating days alternate with days of gray, leaden skies and rains that seep into the earth just before its crust is locked by winter's bitter cold. The northern forests no longer ring with the songs and calls of woodland birds. Many of them have migrated southward, following their age-old instinct to leave long before winter has come.

Summer is gone, and now, with the coming of autumn, it is a season of feverish activity for those earthbound animals that are left behind. Each kind, according to its needs, searches for food, either to be eaten now, or to be stored in preparation for the winter months ahead. The fever of the chipmunks and the tree squirrels is to glean the last seeds and nuts for their supply heaps; the fever of the raccoons, opossums, and skunks seems to be that of eating incessantly—to add layer upon layer of fat upon their bodies as a reserve against the cold and lean times to come.

But this is not the fever of the white-tailed deer. While some of his summer companions of woods and fields—woodchucks and marmots, ground squirrels and jumping mice—have gone underground in the twilight sleep of hibernation, the white-tailed buck knows a fever that rages in him each autumn. For this is the season of the rut—the mating season. It is November.

November finds the buck in all his splendor. His physical condition is the finest of the year. His eyes are bright and alert, his coat is sleek,

and his antlers are his crowning glory.

The breeding, or rutting, season does not come suddenly. It is the result of the gradual releasing of additional hormones into the body system and, with the physiological change, the buck actually trains and prepares himself, much as a boxer would do for a forthcoming fight.

The shedding of the velvet from the buck's antlers is the first outward sign. Then, along about the last of September and the first of October, the buck's neck starts to swell. One beautiful big buck that I measured had a neck circumference of 25¾ inches right behind his ears. The corded neck muscles bulged out on either side into prominent ridges that tapered widely into the shoulders. This thickening of the neck is caused by the development of the muscles, and an increased blood supply brought to the cells.

The buck starts his preparations for the mating season by rubbing the velvet from his antlers, and gradually increases his action until he spends considerable time each day "shadow-boxing," using his antlers to push and hook against resilient saplings and bushes. Young trees that are girdled and gashed by these mock fights can be seen by the hundreds each fall in any countryside well populated by deer.

The bucks usually work over each bush from all sides, even tearing up the earth in a circle around the base. Several times I have seen circles of cleared earth almost two to three feet across where a buck had apparently trampled the earth steadily as he turned his body in a small circle, keeping his forefeet in the same spot.

This constant activity and loss of interest in food rapidly brings down the body weight of the buck. However, he is usually in such good condition before the start of the rut that he doesn't need to eat as much food. Although he may eat sparingly throughout the breeding season, he still has a reserve of fat left in his body in preparation for winter.

The bucks are ready for the breeding season before the does, and are now constantly on the go, seeking mates. Engrossed in their activity, the bucks become less wary and are more frequently seen.

A white-tail buck in the rutting season.

Below, a buck prepares for the rutting season by polishing his antlers. "Buck rubs" like the sapling shown at right are common throughout the woods in the fall.

Autumn

It is during the rut that a buck may actually attack a man or any other creature that he feels is in his way. Although I have never been attacked by a buck in the wild, I have been challenged by one in captivity. One day, as a part of my deer studies, I was taking shoulder-height measurements of some does in a large enclosure. The bucks were penned separately and as I neared the pen containing the largest buck, he snorted loudly. Standing very stiff-legged, he slowly lowered his head, tucking in his chin. This arched his bulging neck and positioned his antlers for battle, to his best advantage. His hair was raised along the crest of his neck and the top of his spine. Slowly he rocked his antlers back and forth, giving vent to an occasional snort. He pawed the earth with his front feet using one foot at a time. I quickly decided not to push my luck or to call his bluff, and walked away.

A buck in the rut is always spoiling for a fight and there is usually another buck ready to oblige him. A buck when fighting does not repeatedly charge headlong into his opponent as do sheep and goats. His fighting method is to put his head against his adversary's and push, at which point the contest becomes one of brute strength as each tries to shove or throw the other off balance. Each keeps constantly on the alert for the opportunity to break out of the headlong push, then get under the other's guard in order to plunge his antlers into his opponent's body. A mature buck usually wins because of superior strength and body weight, although most woodsmen and naturalists with whom I have spoken claim a big spike buck stands a good chance of winning because his long spikes can slip through the branched antlers of the larger deer, and do great damage.

When two evenly matched deer meet in battle the conflict may last for an hour or more. Often the bucks will fight for ten or fifteen minutes or until they are exhausted. Then they stop long enough to get back their wind before resuming the battle.

Sometimes the losing buck may be killed by being gored and trampled; however, most of the time the vanquished one will break off the

69

fight and run away while the victor is content to let him go.

Occasionally when two rack bucks are fighting, their antlers are spread apart by the force of their first impact, only to spring back effectively, locking the two animals securely to one another. It is seldom that bucks thus caught can regain their freedom by their own efforts. The animals with such interlocked antlers are destined to die a horrible death of thirst and starvation, unless they are quickly killed by predators or freed by man. As one or the other of the two bucks becomes weakened and collapses, he effectively shackles his opponent to the spot.

Skeletal remains at right show what might have happened if the two bucks fighting below had locked antlers and been unable to free themselves.

The World of the White-tailed Deer

On several reported occasions men have freed the bucks by sawing off one of their antlers only to have the freed buck turn upon them, so pent-up are some of them with the rage of the fight.

One should never trust a buck in the rutting season, particularly one that has been raised as a pet. Many of these have badly gored and, in some cases, even killed the people who raised them. Deer raised in captivity have lost all fear of man, but in the wild it is this fear which is man's greatest protection against so many of the animals that are larger and much stronger than he is.

A friend of mine who has handled many kinds of wild animals and who maintains a deer park entered one of his pens that contained a large buck. Although the normal rutting season was over, the buck was still aggressive. He attacked without warning, and knocked the man off his feet. Even though my friend kept a strong grip on the buck's antlers to keep from being gored, it was only the intervention of a couple of his hired men that prevented him from being seriously injured or killed.

At the first opportunity the buck was captured and his antlers sawed off. This had the effect of making him peaceable again within a day or so. The removal of antlers or horns from almost any of the males of the big-game, hoofed animals will cause them to lose their belligerence and to become more manageable.

Through most of October the does have been running away from the bucks, which are constantly searching for them. Frequently a buck, with his nose held close to the ground, can be seen trailing a doe by her scent. Although scent plays a far greater role in the lives of wild animals than it does with humans, it is of extreme importance to them during the breeding season.

Both bucks and does have a tarsal gland on the inside of their hind legs. These glands at all seasons give off a very heavy musky odor. It is more pronounced during the breeding season because at that time the deer frequently rub their hind legs together stimulating these glands.

Most of the does mate between the middle of November and the

A buck on the trail of a doe in the rutting season. He picks up scent given off by the tarsal gland (left) inside deer's hind leg.

73

A white-tail doe in her woolly blue-gray winter coat.

middle of December. Those does missed at this time may mate as late as February and this accounts for the fact that fawns with spotted coats are sometimes seen during the following November. (The gestation period of the white-tailed doe is between 200 and 205 days, that is, between six and seven months.) The young of these does seldom live out the winter as they are not large enough or strong enough to survive after cold weather sets in.

The deer in November, in the words of the old-timers, are "in the blue." Starting in early September all of the deer begin to lose their lightweight summer coats of red, which are replaced with the winter

74

coat of gray or slate-blue. The hair of the winter coat is much longer, denser, and each individual hair is crinkled and contains air cells. This hair makes an excellent insulation especially when the deer make it stand on end in much the same manner as a bird fluffing its feathers.

The fawns, too, have shed their russet, dappled coats and are now just smaller editions of the adults. Their protective camouflage is no longer needed because at this time they have grown large enough so that they can outrun most of their pursuers. The two main rows of spots that paralleled the backbone of the fawns may sometimes be carried over into their winter coats. And it is not uncommon to find an occasional adult deer that still shows the same faint rows of spots. Although I have seen deer thus marked on several different occasions I only succeeded in making the one photograph shown below. It was a four-point buck which was at least two and one-half years old.

The World of the White-tailed Deer

A deer has bedded here, its body heat melting the snow beneath it.

The insulating quality of the deer's hair is often demonstrated in the late fall when frozen fog coats everything in the out-of-doors with frost. Every twig and weed appears as a rose bush decorated by the cold with thorns of frost. At such times the deer, too, will be powdered with frost, proving that their body heat loss has been very small. A deer in a snowstorm, bedded down, will melt the snow beneath its body because any escaping heat is trapped by the packed snow and the earth. However, the snow falling upon the upper part of the body will not melt as long as the deer keeps its hair standing on end. The body of a deer that has been shot during a snowstorm will melt the snow as fast as it falls upon it, or until the body heat has been exhausted. This is because the hair in death is laid flat and the dead air is no longer trapped between each hair.

A deer in its winter coat of hair is actually more buoyant in the water as the countless air cells in the hairs act as a life preserver.

Autumn

The hollow hair has one great disadvantage in the fact that it becomes more brittle. Many sportsmen have had deer hides tanned with the hair on to use as throw rugs or a covering for chairs. They are usually disappointed in them because the brittle hairs do not wear well under hard use, and soon break off and fall out.

According to Severinghaus and Cheatham, in their chapter on the white-tailed deer in *The Deer of North America*, melanism (dark-colored or black deer), and true albinism (deer with pure white coats and pink or red eyes) are very rare. "In contrast," they report, "partially white deer are not rare. . . . In New York, for example, three to eight . . . with a

A piebald, or partially white deer.

white-mottled coat appear each year out of a legal take of 12,000 to 30,000 deer. . . ."

The much more common, partially white or partially albino deer is often called a piebald deer. The partly white areas in their coats are not affected by the molt from the winter coat of mixed gray to the summer coat of red, and vice versa. In the molts, the white areas are *always* replaced by white hairs. I was interested to discover that these white hairs in deer are longer than the colored hairs.

The piebald or white-spotted deer are becoming increasingly common, with hunters shooting more of them each season. I believe their increase is a direct result of civilization and of hunting laws. Under primeval conditions in this country, where cougars and wolves abounded, these white-spotted deer would have been more easily seen and hunted harder than would the normal deer, which blend into their surroundings. Where hunting laws do not allow does to be shot, the piebald female deer have a chance to flourish more than in states where both bucks and does can be killed. Many hunters would shoot a piebald doe if they had the chance because the deer's spotted coat makes it an unusual trophy.

Another fact that I have noticed is that white or predominantly white deer seem to have impaired hearing. One local deer that was almost pure white was totally deaf; many people besides myself were able to walk almost up to it while it was in the woods, and it did not hear our approach. It is a little-known fact that most albino mink have proved to be deaf.

The "white" deer are at a further disadvantage in that they are usually avoided by the rest of the deer. The normal deer seem to realize how conspicuous the white deer are and how much more easily they attract unwanted attention to their presence. A few years ago, in the fall, a doe with two almost totally white fawns came frequently to our orchard. The trio became well known and were seen by many, many people. The doe was constantly in attendance on her young but the rest of the herd did not associate with them. I did not see the white fawns the next spring, and can only assume that they perished in the hard winter that had just passed.

One such "white" deer that was in the area several years ago had brown ears. As the ears blended into the background, this deer always seemed earless, this giving her a very comical goat-like appearance.

The deer in the best physical condition are the first to change from their summer hair to the winter coat. The adults usually change before the fawns. However, the time lag is not as noticeable in the fall molting as in the spring because in the fall most of the deer are in top-notch condition.

The favorite food of the white-tailed deer, in areas where they are available, are acorns, with a preference being shown for white-oak acorns over all the other kinds. Anyone who will take the time, as I have done, to taste the meat of the acorns of the various species of oaks will soon agree that the white-oak acorn is the least bitter of them all. When there is a good crop the deer forsake all other types of food, even apples, to stay in the forest and glut themselves on acorns. Feeding as heavily as they can, deer gain their greatest weight in the shortest possible time on this food. The deer and the squirrels are in direct competition for the crop and where the deer herd is large, it may definitely be a controlling factor in the number of squirrels that can live in a given area. Whereas the deer can feed on plant browse and other foods, the squirrel is dependent mainly upon acorns and nuts. Black-oak acorns also rank very high in charts of deer food because, unlike the white-oak acorn, which sprouts and rots in a very short time, the black-oak acorn is available for a longer period.

In addition to acorns, deer seek out and feed upon the nuts of hickory trees, hazelnuts, pecans, chestnuts, and beechnuts. The acorn crop is the most dependable as hazelnuts are rather scarce, and beech trees vary greatly in their productivity from year to year.

Mechanization of our farms, particularly in harvesting grain, has in many ways actually helped deer and other wildlife. An automatic corn picker will miss many ears of corn which would not be left in the fields if the husking were done by hand. This is especially true where some of the cornstalks have been knocked down by strong winds. The deer are quick to find whatever corn is left in the fields and they will feed there each night until the corn is all devoured.

A young buck feeding on fallen fruit in an old apple orchard.

This doe has managed to get a whole apple into her mouth.

Deer also visit truck farms in fall because now that the crops have been gathered, farmers no longer care if the deer feed upon the remaining leaves of cabbages and lettuce.

Apples too are a favorite food of deer, as I have mentioned, and they will seek out the orchards as long as there is an apple available. Not satisfied with the apples that drop off the trees, deer will eat all that they can reach, even standing up on their hind legs to get at the higher fruit. In addition to eating the apples, deer do a rather thorough job of pruning the lower branches by browsing upon them. An adult deer eats an

81

apple either by biting it in half between its incisors and upper jaw, or by taking the whole apple in its mouth and crushing it with its rear molars. While doing this the deer appears to be eating soapsuds, as the apple juice and saliva pour out of its mouth in long sticky strings.

A fawn, being unable to open its mouth that wide, is forced to eat in a daintier manner and must take many small bites from the apple. To prevent the apple from rolling away from it, the fawn backs the apple up against its two front feet and holds it there with its mouth as it eats.

Deer also eat the newly-fallen leaves of the various shrubs and trees. Dogwood, maple, and oak leaves are favorites. Often I have

Deer still grazing where they can in the late fall.

watched deer feeding on leaves as they slowly passed through a second-growth stand of woodland. They prefer the leaves to be freshly fallen and to contain moisture. A leaf that has lain upon the ground for several days is of little interest to them. It has been noted that the moisture content of leaves, twigs, and other foods has a tremendous importance in determining their palatability to deer. The more succulent foods are favored.

Deer at this time of the year can often be seen in large numbers, with some herds totaling up to seventy-five or even more. These concentrations are governed by the availability of food, and are made up of a number of families. Each family group is headed by an older doe and her followers are her offspring and their youngsters. The adult bucks are not with such groups. Such a matriarchal group may have as many as seven or eight members, but seldom more.

Within each family group there is a social organization based upon a pecking order, or dominance system common to almost all of the higher types of living creatures. At the top of this list will be the old doe, who is the actual leader. When feeding, she will take the best food available, which she considers her privilege. The next deer in the social line will have second choice and will yield only to the leader. The third deer in line will chase away all of the other deer in the group but give deference to the number-one and number-two deer. And so it goes right on down the line to the underlings, which feed upon whatever is left.

This system stands up until the family group mingles with a herd. Then the lead doe may chase other deer from the food in order that her entire group may have preference. Often a lead doe will attack an adult buck, forcing him to give way before her.

Over the years, as the lead doe grows old, a younger adult doe may assume the role of leadership, forcing the old doe to a lower level in the pecking order. A crippled or infirm deer is usually at the very bottom of the list and is constantly harassed and picked upon by all of the others.

83

This family group will stay together as long as possible.

There is no sympathy in nature. The rough road to survival forbids it. In a wilderness area, an infirm creature would be eliminated quickly by a cougar, wolf, bobcat, or other large predator. In thickly populated areas, free-running dogs often attack and kill such deer.

Each family group has its own special spot to bed in for the day. Although deer don't seek out the same spot each day, they do bed down in the same general area, weather conditions permitting. In bedding down, deer do not trample the earth in a circle as do wolves, foxes, and other carnivores. They usually select some random grassy or leafy spot and simply lie down. A family group will often bed down within a few feet of one another. This is for safety's sake, as each deer's alertness helps to protect the group.

84

In the spring and summer, deer often bed down in the fields where they feed, particularly if the grasses are high enough to give them some protection. Or they may go back into the shrubby or wooded places. They seldom go any farther from their feeding places than they absolutely need to. In the fall the deer move deeper into the woods, not only because they are seeking more of their food at that time in the forest, but also because the heaviest cover in remote areas provides the best protection during the hunting season. During this season deer abandon their daylight habits almost entirely, and feed under the cover of darkness.

In the hunting season deer seem to be able to tell time. Most states require that a hunter stop hunting about a half hour after sunset. This means that the hunter can usually walk out of the woods before total darkness sets in. During the early bow-hunting season, the deer are still coming out of the woods at night to feed in the fields. As the hunters leave the woods the deer also come out to feed. Many a hunter who hasn't seen a deer all day will leave the woods, get into his car, turn on the lights and be surprised at the number of deer that he sees crossing the road from the woods, returning to the fields to feed.

Deer prefer to follow well-established paths and runways when going to the feeding areas. It probably gives them a feeling of confidence and is important to their safety. Almost every animal will resist efforts to drive it from its home territory. In strange territory it does not know where to seek safety. Then, too, a deer running along a well-known trail knows where each obstacle lies and avoids it. Many deer are injured by sticks and branches in their pell-mell dash for safety when they are surprised and are forced from their runways to escape danger.

Some deer trails have been used for years by countless numbers of deer, so that the trail becomes a rut, particularly when it goes up over the edge of a bank.

Perhaps the most abrupt single change in the life of deer takes place on the opening day of the hunting season. Woodlands, mountainsides, and swamp areas that had previously been left pretty much to the deer are suddenly swarming with men.

The influx of hunters is warning enough to the deer and most of them abandon their more frequently used haunts to seek out safety in the most inaccessible spots they can find. Or, if the cover is sufficient in their regular area, the deer may prefer to stay and play hide-and-seek with the hunters, relying upon their keen senses to keep them from danger.

Many hunters who see deer in certain places during the summer are amazed that they don't see them there in the fall hunting season. A little thought would show them that the movements of hunters radiate from all of the roads in the vicinity. As the hunters leave their cars and advance through the woods, most of the deer simply move on before them. In a section where deer have no real escape territory, they must constantly move out of the hunter's way or hide and let the hunters go past.

Hunters in the deep South often use dogs to hunt deer because of the type of terrain found there. The swamp areas are so extensive and the underbrush so heavy that it is virtually impossible for a man to penetrate the country where the deer seek refuge. Ordinarily, the hunters take "deer stands" on the perimeter of the area to be covered. Selecting well-used deer trails or runways, the hunters hide behind a tree or other cover. When the dogs are released, their course can be followed by their baying and the hunter can easily tell by the dog's excited clamor when a deer has been driven from its bed. If a deer is moving toward a hunter, he had better be prepared to get off a fast snap shot, as the deer will probably be traveling at high speed.

Still-hunting is the most dangerous hunting tactic from the deer's standpoint. In this method, the hunter locates a good deer trail, hides himself on the downwind side, and waits until the deer comes by. By remaining motionless, so the deer doesn't notice him, and by being downwind so that the deer can't smell him, most of the advantages lie with the hunter. However, as most of the northern hunting seasons fall in

November and December, the weather is in the deer's favor, as the extreme cold makes it difficult for the hunters to remain motionless for more than an hour or two. As the hunters become cold they move about, and the deer's chance of locating the hunter first is increased tenfold.

The deer use their trails for a couple of hours after dawn and a couple of hours before sunset. Then, unless there is a large number of hunters in the area to disturb them, the deer lie down and do not use their trails for the rest of the day.

Hunters watching a trail have learned not to be seen by does, or to alarm those that may pass. As the hunting season coincides with the breeding season, there is always a good chance that the does on the trails are being followed by one or more bucks. The buck also may be following the does to allow them to go into each new area first, and to scent danger before he follows. As old does are the natural leaders, it is only to be expected that they will be at the head of the line. The bucks seem to take advantage of this situation for their own self-preservation.

When deer are being tracked and are aware of it, they have a tendency to travel in a circle so that they can get to windward of the hunter, catch his scent and thus locate him more easily. Many hunters, knowing of this habit, will not follow a deer's trail directly but will swing off to the downwind side in large arcs, hoping to get ahead of the deer or to intercept the buck in his circling.

Natural gullies and gaps in a mountain range are very productive hunting spots because all of the various types of game that inhabit the area know of these locations and use them in crossing. Brushy spots lying between the deer's feeding area and their bedding ground will also offer opportunities to the hunter. The deer, being skulking animals by nature, will prefer to follow all cover possible while traveling on their daily routes.

"Jacklighting" or "shining" a deer is another illegal method of hunting deer. Most deer killed by poachers are taken by this method. Automobile headlights are most commonly used in jacklighting, al-

though automobile spotlights and powerful flashlights are also used. The poachers cruise up back roads, visiting spots they know deer frequent. They play their lights over the fields until a beam of light picks up a deer's eye-shine. Apparently blinded or fascinated by the light, the deer usually stands immobile, as in the photographs on the two preceding pages, under the glare of the spotlight.

The poacher then aims his rifle at one of the deer's eyes and fires. If his aim is true, the deer drops immediately. If the deer is not hit in the brain or neck vertebrae, it will probably dash away and so will the poacher. The illegal night hunter just can't afford to search for a deer that runs away, even for a short distance, because the sound of his rifle shot out of season is sure to bring a game warden to investigate, if one is in the area. That is why many of the deer shot at night are not recovered.

Many people claim to be able to tell the sex of a deer by the color of its eye-shine. A doe's eyes are supposed to reflect yellow or red, and a buck's eyes are thought to reflect green. This is not true, in my experience, as I have seen the reflection of a single deer's eyes change color. This is caused when the deer moves its head slightly and the reflective effect of the light on the deer's eye is like that of a changing prism. Red, yellow, orange, and green are the colors most commonly reflected. Many times the eye-shine is the only thing the poacher sees before he fires. Upon investigation, he may find that he has shot some farmer's cow because its eyes reflect light just as the deer's eyes do.

Winter

IT IS cold, bitterly cold. The January and February winds are icy, and over the northern range of the white-tailed deer, the snow often lies deep. There is little moisture in the cold, dry winter air. Distant trees and mountains seem near and are sharply outlined, for the air has a clarity found at no other time of the year. So clear are the night skies that it almost seems one can reach out and gather in the brilliant stars that cluster in myriads in the heavens.

The forest lies silent, its sounds muffled by a mantle of snow. Occasionally the winter silence is shattered by the ripping and groaning of ice on a nearby river, or the resounding crack of a tree split asunder by the cold that knifes into its innermost fibers. Spruces and hemlocks, their snow-laden branches bent to the earth, are nature's "snowmen," motionless and bowed in the swamps and on the forested ridges and hillsides.

In northern Wisconsin, Minnesota, and Michigan, the howling of wolves may pierce the wilderness silence under the stars, for deer are a staple food of the few wolves that still roam some of the wild places of our country. And in the winter silence, the most dreaded sound of all to deer is the yelping of dogs. Big German shepherds and Airedales can kill deer in deep snow just as quickly and savagely as wolves. In New York state, Professor William J. Hamilton, Jr., a well-known zoologist and field naturalist, estimated that in late January alone, dogs kill upward of a thousand snowbound deer. And when deer in winter are confined to a "yard" of their own making, in deep snow, they are especially

There were more than 70 deer feeding in this field at one time, but so widely strung out that only 29 can be seen in this photograph.

vulnerable to attack.

The greatest single factor controlling the size of any deer herd is the availability of winter food. Almost every part of our country where deer live will provide them with an abundance of summer food, enough to support a deer population far in excess of that which can survive in the same area in winter.

Deer movements are seasonal, and correspond to changes in weather. In the northern United States, where the winter snows are usually deep and the weather very cold, the deer shift about more

92

noticeably in autumn in order to adjust to the change in the weather. Deer, which by their natures tend to stay together in small family groups in summer, in winter band together as a herd to survive. Up to 700 deer in New York state have wintered on a south-facing slope two and one-half miles long and a half-mile wide.

In choosing an area to spend the winter, deer may travel to the same nearby swamp, sunny slope of a mountain, or valley, or thicketed bottomland which they have used year after year. In the lowlands, it is dense cover that they seek—white-cedar swamps in Michigan, with possibly a mixture of hardwood trees and shrubs, or swamps of spruce, balsam, and hemlock. In Wisconsin and in the Adirondack Mountains of New York, the wintering area may also be a coniferous swamp. As the snows deepen, deer will leave a good food supply in open areas to find shelter. In the swamps and thickets the shelter is better, deer are protected from wind, and the snows are not so deep. However, food is often scarcer than it is outside the wintering area, because the smaller winter range may be only one-tenth as large as the summer range.

In the North, in winter, deer form a "deer yard." The purpose of such a yard is twofold. Besides protection from the weather, the deer combine to tramp out a network of trails in the swamp over which they can travel to all available food in the wintering area. In mild winters, deer may be yarded for no more than a week or two; in a severe, snowy winter the yarding period may last three to four months. A main disadvantage of the deer yard is the rapid consumption of the food supply.

Another disadvantage is the deer's vulnerability to dogs, wolves, coyotes, and other animals which prey on them. The network of paths or trails in the deep snow allows the deer to run when pursued, but the trails are not long enough to allow them to escape an attacker. And once a deer plunges into deep snow outside the yard, it is helpless. Thus the deer yard may become a dual trap, for by the time the food supply has become low or exhausted, the snow beyond the trails is so deep that the deer, already weakened by starvation, cannot escape, and die within

93

the yard.

This is the reason deer will not, or cannot, move out of the yarding area, even though there may be good food in a swamp or valley only a mile or less away. As Durward L. Allen, a well-known biologist, has said of deer, "They will keep coming back to the same swamp each winter until it's clean—and then leave their bones among the cedars."

Yarding, despite these disadvantages, is still the best means of winter survival in the North. Were it not for yarding of deer, the entire herd might perish during severe snowstorms.

Deer behave somewhat differently where the winters are mild. The nearest approach to yarding in the southern Appalachians is a gathering of deer in coves (large open places in wooded valleys) and on hillsides on which there are thickets of laurel and rhododendron. In central Texas, deer move about very little, either daily or in response to changes in seasons.

In winter, northern deer are forced by necessity to be full-time browsers, because little else is available. Some of the foods they eat are nutritious, others are merely "stuffer foods" on which they gradually starve even though their stomachs are full. The best deer food is usually eaten first and most continuously, until it has been completely eliminated. When this occurs, the deer are forced to eat second-rate or even third-rate foods because nothing else is available. It is this condition of "eat or starve" that causes deer, by eliminating all undergrowth, to change their habitat so that it is no longer habitable to the deer themselves. Songbirds and small forest mammals which depend on trees and shrubs for shelter, food, or for nesting cover also disappear. The "deer line" in overbrowsed forests and swamps plainly marks the stand-up height at which hungry or starving deer feed.

In the northern forest region of New York, New England, Pennsylvania, Michigan, Wisconsin, and Minnesota, white cedar, wherever it grows, is a favorite deer food. So is yew, or ground hemlock, and hemlock trees are also heavily browsed. Hard maple, mountain maple, red

94

The high browse line on the cedars near this deer trail, in a heavily used yard, points to starvation conditions.

The author's son, standing on snowshoes on 30 inches of snow, can just reach the height of the deer browse line on these red cedars.

maple, and striped maple are much eaten by deer in all states where their food habits have been studied.

Oaks, especially in years of a good acorn crop, witch hazel, sumacs, aspens, and yellow and black birch also rank very high in the diet of northern deer. Red cedar and rhododendron, however, in most northern states, are typical of foods on which deer may starve. The winter of 1960–61 was an extremely hard one in the North, with great snow depths and low temperatures. I had the opportunity to examine many

96

Winter

New Jersey deer that had died of starvation. Upon opening their stomachs, I was able to prove to my satisfaction that they had died from eating red cedar. They had consumed all the red cedar available and then, without knowing what was happening to them, had died of starvation although their stomachs were full.

The deer actively sought out the red cedar because I saw their tracks and trails crisscrossing fields, and each trail led directly to a cedar tree. A cedar cut down one day would be stripped of its greenery before dawn of the next day.

Deer that are hungry, and not confined to a yarding area, will move about as much as their strength allows. I have seen hungry deer

Trails leading from one cedar to the next are a pathetic indication of the starving deer's attempts to find browse.

The World of the White-tailed Deer

to whom the angry snarling of a chain saw came to mean food. As soon as the lumbermen would start to cut timber in the morning, the deer came out of the nearby thickets to feed on the twigs and branches of the felled trees. Many times the lumbermen were working on a freshly felled tree while deer were browsing it from the other side.

In Alabama, Arkansas, Missouri, North Carolina, and Ohio, the preferred winter foods of deer are different from those in the North and Northeast. Antennaria, blueberry bushes, Christmas fern, grape vines, greenbrier, or smilax, hazels, mountain laurel, and maples are much eaten, and acorns and oak browse are important deer foods. Green-briers and grasses are much eaten by deer in Texas, and white bay in Mississippi and Louisiana. Deer in the Rocky Mountains prefer pine browse to Douglas fir, and feed heavily on black moss. In South Dakota, bearberry, buckbrush, ceonothus, chokecherry, red osier dogwood, grasses, pines, poplars, and sumacs are much eaten by deer. Deer in Wyoming browse heavily on bur oak, bearberry, Oregon grape, yucca sumac, junipers and western pine.

A browsing deer ordinarily chews off the small twigs (about the size of a lollipop stick) with its front incisors. However, as the food becomes difficult to obtain the deer are forced to eat further back on each branch. Most of this heavy cutting is done with the branch held crosswise in the deer's mouth where the molars can be used. It is seldom that a branch is used that is larger than a lead pencil in thickness. In determining the age of deer by their teeth, scientists often note jawbones that show excessive wear on the molars because of this cutting of branches with the molars.

Deer, unlike many animals such as raccoons, bears and skunks, do not have the ability to store extensive reserves of fat in the body. In a year of plenty when the crops of beechnuts and acorns have been good the deer will accumulate small amounts of fat over the saddle of its back and rump. When a deer can no longer obtain enough food to maintain its body weight because of food shortages, severe weather or hampering

98

A white-tail doe feeding on browse.

A buck using its molars to cut off a branch, when food is hard to find.

snows, malnutrition sets in. If prolonged, the deer begins to starve.

A deer's chest is only eighteen to twenty inches above the ground, and it cannot walk through snow thirty inches deep. When traveling through snow of this depth, the deer must leap over the snow. This requires great exertion and the deer tires very quickly.

When the deer is unable to find enough food to sustain its body weight, self-absorption of the body begins. The fat of the back is absorbed first and then that of the abdominal cavity. When this small supply is depleted the fat that is contained in the marrow of the bones

100

The desperate plunges of a deer in snow almost over its back.

This gaunt doe is near starvation, as shown by her protruding hip bones.

is drawn upon. A well-nourished deer has an almost pure white marrow in its bones that is about 90 per cent fat. This marrow looks just like the white beef suet you buy at the butcher's shop to feed to the birds. As the short ration of food continues, the marrow turns from white to yellow to pink to bright red. This condition denotes a fat content in the marrow of as little as 1.5 per cent. A deer in this condition is going to die even if nutritious food is made available to it. After a deer has lost about one-third of its weight, it seems to reach a point of no return, and death is certain.

Deer suffering from malnutrition become increasingly susceptible to diseases, pneumonia, and predation. They also lose all fear of man mainly because they haven't strength to escape.

Starvation of deer is extremely common, and is worsening each year. A. Starker Leopold, a zoologist at the University of California, has estimated that in a severe winter the nation's loss of deer from starvation may run as high as 2,000,000 animals.

Usually the young deer die first. They are hampered by being smaller, shorter of leg, and having little if any body reserves. It has been recorded in some states that these fawns comprise up to 85 per cent of the total yearly loss.

In a deer yard where food is abundant, all of the deer can feed. As the food supply dwindles, survival of the fittest becomes the rule. The bond between the doe and her fawns has diminished to a point where the doe may drive her own fawns away from food that she needs for herself. As more and more of the lower browse is eaten the fawns, which

A doe in much better condition, probably with fat reserves in her body.

cannot reach as high as the larger adults, can no longer reach anything to eat, and so they die.

The adult females fare better because their size allows them to reach a little higher on the bushes and trees. Nature however has made this period of hardship coincide with the period of the development of the doe's unborn fawns, so that in addition to maintaining her own body requirements, the doe has the added drain of nourishing them. Many in starvation areas give birth to only one fawn instead of the usual pair.

The bucks, which are largest and have no body drain such as the pregnant doe has, fare best of all. Even so, much of the feeding has to be done by the buck standing upon his hind legs to secure food now nearly out of reach. This total consumption of everything within reach often creates a browse line as high as seven feet from the ground.

When browse is no longer available, the deer often resort to bark-stripping, tearing loose all the bark within reach on young trees. This in turn often kills the tree, thereby further reducing the available food for future use.

The body-weight loss of deer under these conditions is tremendous. One very severe winter, while working with our local deer herd, I found a young buck fawn who was so weak he staggered. He had been trying to feed upon some grasses growing in the warmth of a spring hole that was visible from the road. A car came by, the people in it stopped to watch the fawn, and he staggered away into the deep snow. I walked out to where he lay. As I approached he stood up, bawled like a calf, and stumbled forward in my direction. Picking him up, I easily carried him out of the woods and brought him to my home. He was between eight and nine months of age and should have weighed about eighty pounds. He weighed thirty-four. His skin hung in loose folds; his back-bone protruded so sharply that every joint could be felt. He had the typical winter-starved look, with the hair on his head standing on end and giving him a very fuzzy appearance.

The little buck fawn found in the snow by the author, who is shown at left carrying him in.

Although I kept the little buck in a sheltered pen, offered him various types of native browse, grains, commercial feed, and even tried to give him warm milk concentrates, he would not eat. He died five days later. Starvation was too far advanced for him to recover.

Winter

Although deer normally require ten to twelve pounds of browse daily, they can live on as little as two to three pounds. Studies have shown that in extreme cold weather the deer may not even bother to eat at all. The small amounts of food secured by the deer do not compensate for the effort required to obtain it. Then, too, it requires a lot of body heat to thaw out the frozen plant food so that it can be digested. Heat loss is also kept to a minimum by the deer's lying down and staying in one spot after it has that spot warmed. In fact, this may in part explain winter survival.

As I have mentioned, the winter of 1960–61 was the most severe ever recorded in northern New Jersey. Our total snowfall was about sixty-two inches, of which three to four feet lay on the ground most of the winter. Temperatures fell to thirty-five degrees below zero and remained below zero for about three weeks. This produced conditions seldom seen in our state, and approximated that of many of the northern

This deer lay down after the snowstorm was over.

states. In my area we have an estimated total herd of 800 to 1,000 deer scattered over a fifteen-mile-long mountain range. Ordinarily deer are frequently seen crossing the road. I have seen as many as 189 deer within five miles of my home in one hour's time. However, during the cold spell in February, 1961, it was impossible to find a deer moving any place. They had all yarded, and had curtailed all activities. After eighteen days of extreme cold, the weather broke, and by noon the deer were starting to come out of the mountains to seek food on the flats, and along the edges of the fields. Without making an effort to secure an actual count, I later found twenty-eight deer dead of starvation in a reasonably small area and can only assume that this is just a portion of those that perished because of the unusual weather.

Starvation is not only a senseless waste, it is also brought about by man's use of the land, and his failure to keep the deer population within the food-capacity of the land to support just so many deer, and no more.

The white-tailed deer, whose range covers most of the United States, is found in all types of habitat, from suburban areas to the most inaccessible wilderness. The predators which once kept the deer population under control have for the most part disappeared. In North America before our country was heavily settled, when wolves and cougars were numerous, deer lived in large numbers. Although predators held deer within the limits of their food supply—starved deer were easy prey for them—they did not by any means eliminate deer.

In a recent study made over a thirteen-year period in Wisconsin, 2,845 dead deer were examined to discover the causes of death. Only 3 per cent of these dead deer could be blamed upon predators. Predators are inclined to kill the sick, infirm, starved, or crippled animals, simply because they are easier to catch. By eliminating these, predators actually improve the species by leaving most of the healthier, sturdier, more alert ones as breeding stock. Often, where the deer are too numerous for the food supply, predation is helpful in reducing the competition among deer for food. At times, predators benefit deer by preying upon rabbits, hares, mice and other animals that compete with deer for the same plant foods.

By far the greatest destruction of deer by predators is that of domestic dogs. Dogs are the most numerous, often the swiftest and strongest, and the least suspected of predators that kill deer. Many people become incensed when a game protector suspects their dog or dogs of killing deer, yet a pet dog, gentle and affectionate in the house, can become a killer when it runs deer at night.

Deer will run from almost any dog, regardless of its size. All dogs have a hunting instinct and while most of them will chase a deer, possibly for the thrill of it, sooner or later they kill a deer, or join in the kill with other dogs, and become addicted to it.

At one time, cougars and wolves were numerous in the United States, and were probably the main wild killers of deer. Wolves are now so scarce over the range of the white-tailed deer that their effect on the deer population is unimportant. Although cougars are very fond of deer meat (each one may kill an estimated fifty or more deer in a year), they are now generally uncommon over the range of the white-tailed deer, except in Arizona, and other of the Southwestern states. Recently, however, cougars have been coming back in the eastern United States, from Florida to Nova Scotia and the province of New Brunswick in Canada. Where there is overpopulation of deer, and many starve each winter, biologists and game managers are convinced that wolves and cougars would help the deer by keeping their numbers within the capacity of the food supply that will support them.

In studies of the food habits of coyotes in Michigan and Wisconsin, these animals were found generally ineffective as killers of deer, though they often feed on the carcasses of dead deer.

Bobcats, or wildcats, can be effective killers of deer. They live throughout the United States, from southern Canada south to Baja California and into Mexico, from the eastern forests and swamps to the deserts of the Southwest and high in the Rocky Mountains. A bobcat weighing twenty to twenty-five pounds can kill a deer up to the size of a large buck. A game warden in Maine killed one large bobcat (they may weigh as much as thirty pounds) that had killed seven deer that he knew of. The tracks of the bobcat and the carcasses of the deer told the story. The bobcat, like its relative the cougar, or mountain lion, is a silent prowler which makes most of its kills by stalking its prey. A bobcat will usually attack a deer when it is lying down. However, in his Michigan studies, Ilo H. Bartlett concluded that "deer, wolves, coyotes, and bobcats get along well together in Michigan." Bobcats also eat rabbits, mice, hares, and porcupines, which compete with deer for plant foods.

The lynx is much larger than a bobcat and though these big cats subsist largely on hares, it is not difficult for a lynx to overcome a large buck, especially in deep snow. The lynx has become so scarce that it is almost never seen now in the United States. It has a black tip to its tail;

The wolf

The bobcat

The cougar, or mountain lion

the bobcat's tail has its outer edges tipped with white.

I have been a guide for several summers in the province of Quebec, Canada, at the headwaters of the Ottawa River. Our base camp on Lac Landron is just a few miles above the present extreme northern limit for the white-tailed deer. Farther to the south, around Maniwaki, deer are common. The deep snow and the timber wolves are the limiting factors that keep the deer from advancing farther north. Food is not a factor because there is a great deal of good white cedar available as well as other nutritious foods.

Recently many roads have been built in this area to facilitate the removal of pulpwood. Chain saws snarl all day and trucks run day and night. Wolves are heard less frequently and their tracks, once very common, are becoming scarce. As the cut-over area will soon sprout all types of good deer food in tremendous profusion, it is only a question of a year or two until a population explosion of deer will occur in this area. And this condition is being duplicated in many northern sections. The increase in deer numbers will probably prove detrimental to the moose now found there, because white-tailed deer compete with moose for food.

There is an authenticated record of a fox having pulled down a mature deer. This isolated case must be considered an exception to the rule, however, as it would normally be beyond the ability of an eight- to ten-pound fox to kill a 125-pound deer. Foxes may occasionally kill a young fawn, but most of the deer that they eat are undoubtedly carrion. Joseph Taylor, a New Jersey State predator-control man and an authority on foxes, told me recently that in his forty-five years of searching for, and finding, fox dens, he has probably located about 250 of them. A fox with a hungry family has to really hustle to supply enough food for all concerned and consequently will take food it might otherwise pass up. Recently Joe had found the carcass of two fawns in a fox den. This might lead one to believe that the fox had killed the fawns. This was not the case. Both fawns had evidently perished when their mother had been killed on the highway directly in front of the field containing the fox den. Joe knew this because he had removed the doe's carcass five days earlier.

Foxes are very efficient at finding deer carcasses, particularly in the winter. Any fox track in the area will almost invariably lead to a deer killed and lost by hunters, or one that has starved to death. In fact, deer researchers often follow fox tracks in order to find and examine the dead deer in their areas.

The black bear is usually inactive as a predator because it is hibernating at the period when it could be the greatest threat to deer. Black bears usually feed upon winter-killed deer in the early spring when other food is scarce. They may kill a fawn occasionally. The feral hogs of our Southland probably also account for a few fawns. Most of the wild pigs avidly eat any meat available, and they are swift enough to catch a young fawn.

Eagles, particularly the golden eagle, may under favorable conditions attack adult and young deer. Glen Taylor, a hunter for the U.S. Biological Survey, now called the Fish and Wildlife Service, saw a golden eagle in southeastern Arizona attack a fawn of a white-tailed deer. The doe stood up on her hind legs and pawed at the eagle in the air as she attempted to defend her young one. The fawn was lying on the ground under the doe. Taylor shot the eagle and later found that it had injured the fawn, which was almost dead. In contrast, Phillip Wells, of the Arizona Game and Fish Commission, during the spring of 1945 watched a doe white-tailed deer successfully defend her twin fawns against a golden eagle's attack.

In Wyoming in December, 1938, a trapper and his companion watched a large golden eagle swoop down and attack a five-point buck among a small group of mule deer. The eagle caught the deer in the back with its talons, and within a hundred yards, in snow two feet deep, brought it to the ground. Within a few seconds seven more eagles swarmed on the deer and killed it. When the men returned to the area two days later, the eagles had practically devoured the entire carcass, as there were no signs that any other animals had fed upon it.

The U.S. Government report that told of these attacks of golden eagles on deer concluded that "Although the golden eagle will kill either the adult or the young of deer, no evidence was found to indicate that the bird is more than a minor influence when compared to other factors controlling deer populations. . . . Rabbits and rodents form the staple diet of the golden eagle. . . ."

As a general rule, bucks shed their antlers after the breeding season, or from about the middle of December on up till February. If the antlers were grown to be used in defense against predators, they would not fall off in the winter when the deep snows put the deer at their greatest peril.

The bucks in the finest condition and having the largest racks are usually the first to drop their antlers. On many occasions in the New Jersey deer season, which occurs in the middle of December, I have seen bucks that had lost either both antlers or at least one.

Cold is another factor affecting the shedding of antlers. The cooler the season the sooner the bucks seem to drop their antlers. I am not sure whether or not the cold weather moves the mating season forward so that it is completed sooner. It is a positive factor that when the breeding is completed, the antlers are no longer needed and are dropped.

Fred Space, of Beemerville, New Jersey, who has kept a deer herd for a number of years and has made an intensive study of the results of breeding upon antler loss, has come to the conclusion that the more a particular buck is used for breeding the sooner he drops his antlers. To further prove his point Fred has found that where he has penned up a mature buck so that he does no breeding at all, the buck will often carry his antlers into March and April. This seems to give substantial basis to the evidence that the older, larger bucks shed their antlers first. But this is another area where much deer research remains to be done in order to eliminate conjecture and replace it with fact.

The buck's antlers become whiter as they are bleached by sun and weather.

Diet also is a factor in antler loss. As has already been mentioned, bucks on a poor diet grow their antlers late, shed the velvet late, and drop the antlers late.

How do the deer actually shed their antlers? I have been told and also have read reports that the deer are supposed to remove their antlers by knocking them against some hard object such as a tree. I discredit all such accounts. When it is the right time for the antlers to fall off, they fall off. It is virtually impossible to knock off an antler before the proper time. Bucks by the thousands, after being killed in the hunting season, are dragged by the antlers and if properly hung up for dressing and aging are hung by the antlers. The bucks themselves fight with trees, fences, and each other, using tremendous force, without knocking off the antlers. On one occasion when Fred Space was attacked by a large captive buck he hit the buck a powerful blow on the antlers with a piece of iron pipe, hoping to knock them off. Although the blow was forceful enough to knock the buck unconscious the antlers were not even loosened.

Occasionally in the hunting season, an antler receives a direct hit from a ball or bullet. Then the antler will shatter or break from the impact. If on a rare occasion the antler breaks off at the base, it is only because it was ready to drop off anyway.

I once found a set of antlers lying on the ground where the buck must have stood while both antlers fell off simultaneously. This seldom happens. It is much more common for antlers to fall off one at a time. Bucks are often seen with a single antler, having lost the other.

When the antler falls off it breaks free right below the burr of the antler, leaving the pedicel, which is a part of the deer's skull. The pedicel thus exposed has a moist red surface looking exactly like a human sore that has had the scab knocked off. Very little or no bleeding accompanies this loss. The pedicel stays quite raw-looking for three to five days, when it begins to scab over and gradually dries up.

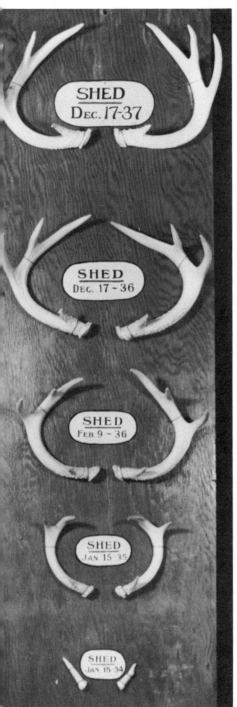

The buck at top, above, has just lost his antler; the pedicel is still raw. After several weeks, below, the pedicel has healed over, and new antler growth can begin.

The sets of antlers at left were shed by the same deer, held in captivity by Fred Space, over a period of four years.

A buck which has lost one antler.

Many hunters are not aware that bucks shed their antlers, simply because the hunters have never found the shed antlers in the woods. The frequency with which they are found, of course, is also governed by the number of deer in the area.

As the months go by the antlers become harder to find. For long periods they may be covered with leaves and then with snow. During this time, wild mice and other animals are busily gnawing upon the antlers because of their high content of calcium and phosphorus. By summer most of the antlers have been consumed and their minerals have become a part of some other creature's body.

118

Rodents have gnawed these antlers.

Deer and Men

IT IS impossible to discuss deer without discussing deer management, because there is scarcely a deer alive in America today that is not directly influenced by man. Man controls the water the deer drinks, the food that it eats, the land that it lives on, and he regulates the manner, season, and sex of the deer harvested. And harvest the deer he must because they have become a crop of the land in the same sense as the food we eat. That man, in his faltering way, does not always manage the deer crop in the best manner can readily be seen by the problems confronting many states.

It is exceedingly difficult to estimate just how many deer there were in what is now the United States before the coming of the white man. Deer thrive best on cut-over forest lands, and because most of our good, present-day deer country was still in virgin timber, there were much smaller numbers of deer 200 years ago than we are accustomed to see today. The United States Fish and Wildlife Service, using the most up-to-date census methods, estimates our present white-tailed deer population in this country at more than 5,000,000 animals.

As the early settlers cut down the forests, and deer food increased, deer population began to rise. In order to protect his cattle, horses and sheep, the settler waged increasing war on the larger predators, which also protected deer. As the deer increased, they moved onto the settler's land and ate his crops. Deer damage to crops goes back to the earliest record of farm crops in this country.

The settlers hunted deer for food, and deer hides became a standard item of barter. Then large-scale lumbering in the 1800's caused the deer population to skyrocket. This also ushered in the day of the market hunters, whose heavy toll of deer caused the population to plummet downward. Uncontrolled forest fires, wiping out millions of acres of deer food, also reduced herds. Much of the early tree and shrub growth, which followed the heavy lumbering, soon grew out of the deer's reach. Together these factors combined to produce an all-time low in the deer population at the turn of the century.

Although some laws had been passed to protect deer, many people now clamored for better laws, more rigidly enforced. Slowly but surely the pendulum reversed its swing and the deer population began an accelerating rise.

A deer today is its own worst enemy. They have so increased that in many areas they suffer annually from chronic starvation. "Bucks only" laws passed years ago to help in re-establishing the dwindling deer herds now work against the deer by resulting in an overabundance of does which can't legally be killed. Many hunters, not clearly understanding the situation, have insisted that these laws remain in effect, and when they band together in sportsmen's federations the pressure they exert on state officials prevents game managers from accomplishing the job for which they have been trained and hired. If sensible liberalized hunting laws are passed, many of these same hunters will still refuse to shoot a doe. They believe in the old saying, "It takes a doe to yield a buck." This is true, but it ignores the basic law of nature that any piece of land, and the food and cover on it, can support only so much game. If the excess game is not killed by man or predators, it is killed by nature with its efficient weapons of disease and starvation.

I believe that more attention should be given to the staffing of the various state game commissions by trained and experienced wildlife technicians instead of political appointees. These commissions should then be allowed to operate unhampered by the various pressure groups, composed oftentimes of sportsmen and farmers. These commissions would be aware that if they do not pursue the wisest management course, they will have no game to manage and thus no jobs.

A game census is accomplished by different methods of varying reliability. One of the most common and most accurate today is the counting of deer actually seen against a snow background by game biologists in a low-flying helicopter. Although this has a high per-hour cost it is probably one of the cheapest methods for the quick and accurate results it allows.

Counting deer by "deer drives" is also employed regularly by many of the states. Other states require all of their men working in the field to keep records of all game seen daily crossing various roads.

Deer populations may be measured by pellet (dung) counts, either (where this can be done) on the first day after a snowstorm or on a long-term basis by counting them after the leaves fall in autumn and before the snow comes. In many states deer killed by hunters must be tagged. This is another important census method and one now almost universally in use.

Counting deer is very important, for the deer managers must have some idea of how many deer are available in order to formulate the proper length of the hunting season, the opening date, and the allowable kill. In order to control the size of the herds, some areas need more hunting than others and a census is the only reliable way to obtain this information.

Deer are trapped in order that they may be ear-tagged so that accurate records can be kept on specific deer. By retrapping the same deer, home ranges can be charted, growth rate and weight can be studied, longevity determined, and many other observations of their life can be made. Recently chemical dart guns have been used to temporarily paralyze the deer so that a live examination can be made. So far, these guns are not as practical as claimed. All too often, the deer may die from an overdose of the chemical, or because it has been hit in an especially vulnerable spot.

Deer and Men

Deer are also trapped to alleviate overpopulation in sanctuaries. Removing deer from overpopulated areas in the wild is seldom practical because it is too time-consuming and costly. Moreover, there is rarely an area where the trapped deer can be released which is not already overpopulated.

Deer trapping has an added drawback in that it can only be managed on a large scale in the winter when deer are hungry enough to be tempted by the baited trap. Most deer traps are of the common box-trap type and do not injure the trapped animals. Recently several of the states have tried trapping deer by using large rubber-band snares. These have not been generally successful.

"Feed them with an ax" is a widely used slogan based on good conservation principles. In many areas where the trees have reached maturity and have grown beyond the deer's reach, the felling of trees or lopping off of branches will help supply needed food. Red maple in particular, a good deer food, can be cut back time after time. This will cause the stump to grow "suckers," or leafy upright stems which produce a tremendous amount of food.

At left, red maple sprouts which have been heavily browsed, but will continue to yield good deer food. The "bean-pole" woodland at right has grown beyond the deer's reach.

The World of the White-tailed Deer

Aspen and some of the birches (not black birch) are trees that are seldom used commercially and can be sacrificed for food. In felling trees for food, they should be cut only part way through, and never all the way around. In this manner the tree will continue to grow even after the top is down so that the deer can browse on it. I have often gone out on snowshoes in the winter to deer yards to cut trees in this manner. Deer can usually browse on the tree for about ten years before it grows too high, but it usually takes another twenty to twenty-five years before the tree can be harvested commercially.

Controlled burning to increase the growth of underbrush is too hazardous and too destructive to the forest, although it is still practiced in some parts of the country. The Indians used to burn over areas in order to increase the underbrush and new growth, thus insuring them of a handy supply of venison when it was needed. Not only is there a chance of the fire getting out of hand, but much of the mulch and forest topsoil burns up too.

Bulldozing clearings in the middle of mature stands of trees will induce heavy new growth, and is being done more extensively.

The big drawback to these forest management problems is that often the deer are not as valuable as the timber that is destroyed to feed them. Each situation must be carefully evaluated. In many areas the deer have destroyed entire reforestation efforts. They not only eat everything already planted but make it impossible to plant any additional trees because of their regular feeding. In some rare cases, deer browsing, if not too severe, has actually benefited the forest because it is very much like the pruning that man does to trees to encourage greater growth.

Cutting trees for deer can usually be done only on state-owned lands. Most private owners depend on their forest or woodlot as a potential cash crop. If the demand for wood products is high, both state and private landowners are going to be cutting trees anyhow to meet the market requirements. When the demand is low little timber will be

124

harvested and the deer will not have the additional available food supply of the lopped branches from felled trees.

Food patches planted for deer will provide additional supplemental food. I have found that rape is an excellent winter food. Deer will paw down through two feet of snow to browse the plant off at ground level. Diversionary food patches are often planted in an effort to lure deer away from some domesticated crop where they are doing damage. Cow peas, buckwheat, and particularly soy beans, make excellent food-patch plantings for deer.

Each winter, when the snows pile up, the temperature drops, and the first reports of deer starvation trickle in, sympathetic people and many sportsmen believe we should feed deer. Tons of timothy hay, stale bread, and cabbage greens are hauled out to the edges of woods and dumped off. However, more deer have been killed by eating timothy hay than ever were saved by it. Most of the bread and the greens go untouched and the bulk of it is usually dumped out where the deer can't

Winter feeding of deer (left) is only a stop-gap method. At right, a hole eaten into the earth by deer, who will consume soil for the sake of the salt it contains.

The World of the White-tailed Deer

reach it anyway. Deer cannot subsist on timothy hay, although they do like the weeds that are usually mixed with this hay. In winter feeding experiments of wild deer in Wisconsin, hundreds of thousands of dollars were spent before it was discovered that the nutritional requirements of deer are not satisfied by a diet of hay. Deer will eat good alfalfa and clover hays, and many of the states have developed concentrated deer food rations. However, the cost of the food, the cost of transporting it, and the cost of manpower are so high that it becomes impractical. It is not possible to feed all the deer, and even if it were, instead of easing

A white-tail doe being fed on corn.

winter starvation, artificial feeding compounds the problem instead. It may save some deer, but in doing so, only adds more to the already over-burdened range. To solve the problem, deer populations should be reduced, before winter sets in, to the approximate number of deer that can winter on the range within the limits of their natural food supply.

It has been estimated that each year the value of venison eaten by American families runs into millions of dollars. Many millions are spent on guns, ammunition, licenses, hunting clothing, gasoline, food, lodging, guides, and all the other needed accessories to hunting. Many communities in "deer country" derive the bulk of their income from deer hunting and the hunters. All of these things can actually be tallied up with a dollar and cents value, but how do we put a price on aesthetic value? Countless millions of people gain an equal amount of pleasure simply in seeing a deer. Some of the most enjoyable times of my life have come when I have been able to sit quietly in the woods and fields, observing deer as they have gone about their daily lives unaware of my presence. I know many others who feel as I do.

As the white-tailed deer differs from the mule deer in both internal and external characteristics, we also find a remarkable difference between the various subspecies of the white-tailed deer. Many of these differences are conspicuous. Size of the animal, color variations, and the differences in antler development are among the most noticeable features. Where the ranges of some of these geographical races of the white-tailed deer meet, one subspecies may blend almost imperceptibly into another, particularly where there are no abrupt changes of climate and geography. Then, too, in the early days of our interest in increasing deer, many were transported from their home ranges for restocking on the range of another subspecies. Where this has been done, the deer have interbred and the resulting crosses, or hybrids, made it impossible later for taxonomists positively to classify some of them either as one subspecies or another. Where the plains or deserts meet high mountains,

The World of the White-tailed Deer

however, and there are sharp differences in the country itself, the sub-species of deer that occupy these areas are generally markedly different.

In North America and Central America, from Hudson Bay, Canada, south to the Isthmus of Panama, there are thirty subspecies or varieties of the white-tailed deer. Seventeen of these live within the continental United States, and those living in the northern states are, on the whole, the largest. The white-tailed deer tend to become smaller farther south, with the Florida Key deer the smallest of all subspecies in the eastern United States. The deer living at the highest altitudes tend to be darker in coloration; those of the dry plains or desert are more lightly colored. Their common and scientific names and distribution are as follows:

1. The northern white-tailed deer, *Odocoileus virginianus borealis,* is probably the best known of all the deer. It has the greatest distribution, which includes most of the best deer-hunting states such as Pennsylvania, New York, Maine, Wisconsin, and Michigan. Its range extends from James Bay in Canada south to Illinois, west to Minnesota and east to the New England states and the Canadian Maritime Provinces. This deer is one of the largest subspecies and the males usually develop the finest trophy heads.

2. The Dakota white-tailed deer, *Odocoileus virginianus dacotensis,* lives in the Dakotas, Nebraska, Wyoming and Montana. It is most frequent in the coulees and draws that break up these prairie states. Most of the water courses are tree-lined and provide good cover for the deer. Late in the evening and early morning, they may be seen out on the open flats browsing upon the various shrubs.

3. The northwest white-tailed deer, *Odocoileus virginianus ochrourus,* lives in Washington, Oregon, Idaho, Wyoming, and Montana. There, in the heart of the mule deer country, the white-tail will be found in the heaviest brush whereas the mule deer prefers the more open bench land.

128

Odocoileus virginianus ochrourus

The World of the White-tailed Deer

One of the largest bucks I have ever photographed was the one on the preceding page, which I flushed out of heavy clover in Glacier National Park while I was looking for moose.

4. The Columbia white-tailed deer, *Odocoileus virginianus leucurus,* lives in small pockets of its range scattered along the coast of Oregon and Washington. The range of this deer is shrinking, and it becomes fewer in number as the years go by. There are probably less than a thousand of these deer alive today.

5. The Virginia white-tailed deer, *Odocoileus virginianus virginianus,* was the deer first seen and recorded by the early settlers of the Virginia colonies. Its range extends from south of the Ohio River, bordered on the west by the Mississippi River, and includes all of our states of the Deep South.

6. The Florida white-tailed deer, *Odocoileus virginianus seminolus,* lives from southern Georgia southward to the Florida Keys.

7. The Florida coastal white-tailed deer, *Odocoileus virginianus osceola,* lives on the Gulf coast of Alabama and Mississippi. It is a medium-sized deer and considerably paler in coloration than the Virginia white-tailed deer.

8. McIlhenny's deer, *Odocoileus virginianus mcilhennyi,* or the Avery Island white-tailed deer, is found only along a narrow strip of southern Louisiana and Texas bordering on the Gulf of Mexico.

9. The Kansas white-tailed deer, *Odocoileus virginianus macrourus,* lives west of the Mississippi River in Iowa, Kansas, Missouri, Arkansas, Louisiana, Oklahoma and Texas. The range of this animal is shrinking as deer of the other subspecies tend to overlap and intergrade with them.

10. The Texas white-tailed deer, *Odocoileus virginianus texanus,* inhabits western Texas, New Mexico, Colorado, Oklahoma, and southward into Mexico bordering the Rio Grande. Its range formerly extended farther northward. Although not as large as our northern whitetails, *texanus* is the largest deer to inhabit any part of Mexico.

11. For many years it was thought that the small Coves' white-tailed deer, or the Arizona white-tail, *Odocoileus virginianus couesi,* was a distinct species of white-tailed deer. Today, however, it is considered to be a subspecies. One of the outstanding characteristics of this deer is its exceptionally large ears, giving it a mule deer look.

12. The Carmen Mountains white-tailed deer, *Odocoileus virginianus carminis,* has a very small range in the United States in the Big Bend region of Texas and along the Rio Grande River.

13. Bulls Island white-tailed deer, *Odocoileus virginianus taurinsulae,*

14. Hunting Island white-tailed deer, *Odocoileus virginianus venatorius,*

15. Hilton Head Island white-tailed deer, *Odocoileus virginianus hiltonensis,* and

16. Blackbeard Island white-tailed deer, *Odocoileus virginianus nigribarbis*

are four subspecies of deer that are found on the Atlantic coastal islands of Bulls Island, South Carolina, Hunting Island, South Carolina, Hilton Island, South Carolina, and Blackbeard Island, Georgia, respectively, one subspecies to each island. Although some deer could cross to the mainland or to other islands they apparently do not do so. Living isolated as they do and have done for such a long period of time, the subspecies have evolved distinct differences among themselves and are different from those of the mainland.

The World of the White-tailed Deer

17. Of all the subspecies, perhaps the one to generate the greatest interest and concern is the diminutive Florida Key deer, *Odocoileus virginianus clavium*. These tiny creatures, smallest deer in the United States, live only on Big Pine Key and a few of the smaller surrounding Keys. In the early days they frequently traveled from one Key to another. Hunting by men and dogs and hurricanes have virtually exterminated them. Today the United States Government has established a Key deer refuge in Monroe County, Florida, where it is hoped that the present estimated seventy-four deer will survive and thrive.

An unusual phenomenon of the Key deer is that, living in an area that knows no seasonal changes, they have no definite time for molting their coats, or growing and dropping their antlers. They have a year-round breeding season so that the fawns may be born in any month of the year.

It has often been said that the last creature to survive on this earth will probably be an insect. However, the white-tailed deer, which has outlived such early predators as the saber-toothed tiger, diseases, starvation, hunting, and mismanagement, seems a likely possibility as a chief competitor for the last remaining herbage on earth.

Bibliography

Allen, Durward L., "Does Ain't Deer," *Sports Afield,* 120 (6) (1948), pp. 19–21; 90–91.

Audubon, John James and Bachman, John, *The Viviparous Quadrupeds of North America* (J. J. Audubon and V. G. Audubon, New York, N. Y., 1846–1854).

Banasiak, Chester F., *Deer in Maine* (Department of Inland Fisheries and Game, Augusta, Me., 1961).

Cahalane, Victor H., *Mammals of North America* (Macmillan, New York, N. Y., 1947).

Dahlberg, Burton L. and Guettinger, Ralph C., *The White-Tailed Deer in Wisconsin* (Wisconsin Conservation Department, Madison, Wisc., 1956).

Gregory, Tappan, *Deer at Night in the Northwoods* (Charles C. Thomas, Baltimore, Md., 1930).

Hamilton, William J., Jr., *The Mammals of the Eastern United States* (Comstock Publishing Company, Ithaca, N. Y., 1943).

Jenkins, David H. and Bartlett, Ilo H., *Michigan Whitetails* (Michigan Department of Conservation, Lansing, Mich., 1959).

Latham, Roger M., *Pennsylvania's Deer Problem* (Special issue No. 1, Pennsylvania Game Commission, 1950).

133

Bibliography

Leopold, Aldo, "Deer Irruptions," *Transactions of the Wisconsin Academy of Science, Arts, and Letters,* 35 (1943), pp. 351–66.

Merriam, C. Hart, *The Mammals of the Adirondack Region* (Published by the author, New York, N. Y., 1884).

Miller, Gerrit S. and Kellogg, Remington, "List of North American Recent Mammals," *U. S. National Museum Bulletin,* No. 205 (Smithsonian Institute, Washington, D. C., 1955).

Nelson, E. W., "The Larger North American Mammals," *National Geographic Magazine,* November, 1916.

Newsom, William M., *Whitetailed Deer* (Scribner, New York, N. Y., 1926).

Seton, Ernest Thompson, *Lives of Game Animals* (Doubleday, Doran, New York, N. Y., 1929).

Taylor, Walter P., ed., *The Deer of North America* (The Stackpole Company, Harrisburg, Pa., and The Wildlife Management Institute, Washington, D. C., 1956).

Warren, Edward R., *The Mammals of Colorado* (Putnam, New York, N. Y., 1910).

Young, Stanley P., *The Bobcat of North America* (The Stackpole Company, Harrisburg, Pa. and The Wildlife Management Institute, Washington, D. C., 1958).

Young, Stanley P. and Goldman, Edward A., *The Wolves of North America* (The American Wildlife Institute, Washington, D. C., 1944).

——, *The Puma, Mysterious American Cat* (The American Wildlife Institute, Washington. D. C., 1946).